BOXES AND HOW WE FILL THEM
A Basic Guide to Sexual Awareness
Kristen Lilla, LCSW, CST, CSE, CSTS, CSES

Sex Ed Talk LLC
Omaha, NE

This paperback original is published by
Sex Ed Talk LLC Omaha, NE
www.sexedtalk.com

1st Edition
ISBN 978-1-7329132-1-9

Library of Congress Cataloging-in-Publication Data is on file.

Cover Design by Athena Currier
Book design by Michael Campbell, MC Writing Services

What others say about Boxes and How We Fill Them

"Kristen is an enthusiastic sex educator and compassionate therapist who knows how to blend modern sexuality science with tried-and-true therapeutic practices. She's always on the cutting edge of sexual health, and she's a great role model for anyone looking to enhance their sensual relationship—with a partner, or with themselves."

Colleen Godin, journalist and consultant for the sexual wellness industry

"One has to know the author to know how smart, practical and easy to read this book is. Kristen takes complex subjects and makes them easy to understand. This book is great to help readers have a framework for having complex discussions about sex with the important people in their life. The exercises at the end of each chapter are fun and great prompters for further discussion. If you want more sexual awareness in an easy to digest format, this book is for you."

Neil Cannon, Ph.D., LMFT, AASECT Certified Sex Therapist and Supervisor

"I have long admired Kristen Lilla as someone who has a pulse on the priorities of the field of sexuality, and as someone who puts her heart and soul into the well-being of others."

Bill Taverner, MA, CSE, Chief Editor, *American Journal of Sexuality Educator*

"Written with clarity and compassion, Boxes and How We Fill Them *is nothing less than essential reading. Lilla expertly draws on a wealth of experience to offer readers context for a broad range of topics in the field of sex and sexuality, presenting easy-to-follow exercises that put healing, expanding, discovering or rediscovering our sexual selves within reach. It's difficult to imagine a reader whose life would not be positively impacted by this book."*

Grant Stoddard, Co-Author of *Great in Bed*

"In your hands is a product of her zeal: blending theory, narrative, and training, this book is a dialogue with the reader that is playful, engaging, and still a deeply informative guide through technique, communication, awareness of one's own needs and the connection to one's body, kink, ability/disability, fantasy, and other topics as well."

Laura A. Jacob, LCSW-R, Co-Author of *You're in the Wrong Bathroom!*

BOXES AND HOW WE FILL THEM

A Basic Guide to Sexual Awareness

. . .

Kristen Lilla

To Dylan, I love you mostest monkey

To Drew, I love you super much

■ ■ ■

CONTENTS

PREFACE

The topic of sexuality is my passion. I love talking about sexuality, educating others about sex, and helping people work through their sexual issues. Ultimately, I aim to empower others to take control of their sexuality.

Growing up, I was a free spirit and was raised in a supportive home. I was inquisitive and asked my parents many questions about sexuality over the years. My parents offered an answer to my questions, perhaps begrudgingly, but always honestly. Like most youth, I also learned a lot about sexuality from my peers.

When I was a senior in high school I saw The Vagina Monologues, a play by women's rights activist Eve Ensler. Ensler traveled the world asking women about their sexuality and vaginas. She compiled their stories, a collection of monologues, ranging from hilarious to heart-wrenching, and included topics about sexual assault and masturbation. When I saw the show it was the first time issues related to women's sexuality were spoken about without me having to ask. The show portrayed women receiving, and being deserving of, sexual pleasure. It was also the first time the issue of sexuality was put on a platform. I didn't want the show to end. More importantly, I didn't want the conversation to end.

When I started college, I wanted to be a pharmacist, like my dad. However, it became apparent very quickly that I did not excel at calculus or chemistry, so I decided to pursue a degree in psychology. So without another thought I changed majors and decided to become a sex therapist. *Is that even a real job?* I questioned. I wondered if I had made it up. After doing some research I discovered AASECT, the American Association for Sexuality Educators, Counselors, and Therapists. I had discovered another platform to have discussion around sexuality since *The Vagina Monologues*. At age 19 I reached out to get more information, and become a student member of the organization. I haven't looked back since.

Through my journey to become a sex therapist, I learned how complex sexuality and sexual issues could be. Now people come into my office on a daily basis to discuss their relationships, intimacy, and sexual issues. Sex therapy is a specialty in therapy that focuses on intimacy and relationship issues. It often goes hand-in-hand with marriage and couples counseling, but I'm trained and qualified in areas of sexuality so I can assist couples with issues related to intimacy as well. Sometimes people come in for therapy by themselves, sometimes with their partner, sometimes with more than one partner. They may come for one session just to get feedback, permission, or education. Other people may engage in therapy over the course of months or years if their issues are more complex.

I have presented professional workshops locally, nationally, and internationally, including multiple presentations at the National Sex Education Conference and the annual American Association of Sexuality Educators, Counselors, and Therapists Conference. The workshops I present always include a strengths-based approach. It is imperative that people realize the inner strength they have to overcome their issues, to take care of themselves, and to empower themselves to have a rich and fulfilling sex life.

As you can see, my passion has not waned. I continue to learn and grow and ask questions—I just have a lot more answers now than I used to, and I want to share them with others. I hope you enjoy *Boxes and How We Fill Them: A Basic Guide to Sexual Awareness*.

INTRODUCTION

Imagine that every lesson learned, success, and regret are all put into different boxes. These boxes are your life experience. Within these boxes are messages you received about sex, gender, and body image. Some of the boxes contain experiences that inform how you communicate, like your first love story or a devastating break-up. Each story is put into a box.

This book will help you determine how your boxes were filled throughout your lifetime. It will help identify which messages you held onto and put in a box stacked high on a shelf, and which messages are in boxes wide open and ready to be used.

Go through the book and consider all of your boxes and how you filled them over the years. As you unpack your boxes, throw some away, recycle them, or create new ones, you will start to develop basic tools for communication and sexual awareness in your own life.

While this book is *not* a replacement for therapy, it *is* dedicated to helping the reader confront issues related to sexuality, engage in self-care, and be empowered. This book addresses a variety of sexuality issues I work with as a therapist. Each chapter summarizes a topic and offers approaches to working through the issue discussed. In therapy I aim to identify the problem and help resolve the issue by offering tools and resources to clients. This book shares many of those tools.

The first session in therapy is spent processing intake paperwork, reviewing medications, learning relationship status, and discussing the presenting problem. As clients share their story and their goals for therapy, I start to tease out what contributed to the problem and rule out things the client has already tried. It serves to lay the groundwork for what is to come next in therapy.

Throughout therapy I try to offer exercises and resources to clients. It is important to me that clients work on issues outside of therapeutic sessions, and most of my clients find the suggestions valuable.

Since sex therapy tends to be solution-focused (meaning that we're working towards fixing a specific problem) I want to help clients establish therapeutic goals. My hope is to help clients have the proper tools in their toolbox to work through issues, learn to regulate emotions, and improve communication. This is not to say that issues never return after terminating therapy, but a person should have the tools they need to tackle the issue hands-on without coming to therapy again for the exact same reason. When people do choose to come back to therapy—and many do re-engage in therapy after a few months or years—it is to gather additional resources or resolve new issues. Typically, the time spent in additional therapy is shorter because they are already equipped with resources to start tackling the problem.

This book is broken up into 26 chapters, each dedicated to a specific topic. You may choose to read this book in its entirety, or you may select the chapters you feel are most applicable to you. However you decide to approach the book, feel free to read it in sequential order or jump around. Each chapter discusses a problem, includes at least one case study, offers general advice and recommendations, and concludes with at-home exercises. Many chapters throughout the book reference one another, and the exercises are often adaptable to a variety of situations. You may find chapters you don't think are relevant to your situation include exercises and tools that are.

The book will discuss important relationship concepts such as communication, vulnerability, and sexual scripts. It will discuss physical issues including erectile dysfunction and vaginal pain. As you read, explore concepts that may be new to you, such as kink and sexual fantasy. Go through each chapter with an open mind, and determine how you have filled boxes on each subject and how you can recycle and recreate those boxes.

Again, this is a self-help book. Each of the 26 chapters offers a great place to start identifying your issues. I hope it empowers you and provides you with the tools you need to unpack your boxes. However, it is also important to note that reading a book or trying to solve an issue on your own may not be enough. This book can also help you decide if you need the help of a professional.

If seeking professional help would benefit you, I suggest you to see an AASECT Certified Sex Therapist by searching for a professional where you live (aasect.org). AASECT holds its professionals to rigorous standards of professional training, development, consultation, and supervision in the field, ensuring their expertise in treating sexuality issues.

■   ■   ■

COMMUNICATION

Communication often means having a conversation with someone where we share our thoughts and feelings, but we communicate in many other ways, including verbally (verbal), through physical touch (nonverbal), via body language (visual), or written on paper, like this (written).

About 60–70% of our communication tends to be through touch. While this is useful, it is not always direct and can be misread by others. This is a pattern that happens frequently between couples. When miscommunications like this occur, I gently remind clients their partner cannot read their mind. Additionally, almost all verbal forms of communication are paired with other forms. For example, if I ask you to take out the trash in a pleasant tone (verbal), intended as a favor, while I am giving you a hug (nonverbal), it will be perceived very differently than if I ask you to take out the trash (verbal) while I roll my eyes (visual) and point at the trash can (visual). At the end of the day, communication is all we have to rely on. When couples stop communicating, they can expect their relationship to suffer.

When couples really struggle with miscommunications and fighting, I introduce them to John Gottman's concept of the Four Horsemen of the Apocalypse: criticism, contempt, defensiveness, and stonewalling. Gottman is a world-famous marriage therapist based out of Seattle. While he has not been a large contributor to the world of sex therapy, he has a lot of well-researched information and knowledge for couples to utilize.

Gottman has been studying married couples for over 25 years. His first study in 1992 provided him with enough data and information about couples and how they argue to be able to predict divorce with a 91% accuracy rate. He noticed a trend among couples whose marriages ended in divorce as they engaged in unhealthy patterns of fighting. These four distinct patterns became known as The Four Horsemen of the Apocalypse.

Gottman got the name from the Bible, in the Book of Revelation 16:1–8. Christians have interpreted this passage to indicate that an apocalypse will occur. Gottman named his theory after this concept, forcasting that couples who engage in his Four Horsemen will find themselves at the end of their relationship.

The first of the Horsemen, *criticism,* is beyond the point of complaining or venting. It includes calling a partner names, pointing out their inadequacies, and placing blame. Gottman says one of the most jarring criticisms is asking a partner, "What is wrong with you?" (Gottman, 1999, p.28).

While *defensiveness* is a natural response to someone who is attacking us, Gottman explains it "rarely has the desired effect" (p. 31) because the person attacking is not likely to back off, and in turn is likely to become defensive themselves. As you can imagine, the second of the Horsemen results in a vicious cycle with no resolution.

Another concept is *stonewalling,* which is similar to withdrawing or shutting down. Stonewalling is much more common among men than women, as Gottman discovered in his research. Common reactions among people who stonewall include ignoring their partner, avoiding eye contact, looking down or away, and remaining silent (Gottman, 1999).

Contempt is the final of the Four Horsemen. It is the biggest predictor of divorce, as Gottman has come to find out through his years of marital research. Contempt can rear its ugly head in a variety of forms both verbal and non-verbal. Verbally, it includes sarcasm and cynicism. Non-verbal contempt can include eye rolling and sneering. It is the most dangerous of the Four Horsemen because it "conveys disgust" and "it's virtually impossible to resolve a problem when your partner is getting the message you're disgusted with him or her" (Gottman, 1999, p. 29). As with the other Horsemen, engaging in contempt will only lead to more conflict rather than any discussion or resolution.

Case study: Kendall and Sheldon

Kendall, a black gay man in his late 30s, was working as a real estate agent. He set up a therapy appointment for himself and his partner, Sheldon. At their session, Kendall spoke freely. He shared that he had been with Sheldon, a web developer, for six years. They met while living in Chicago through a mutual friend. Kendall reported that they "clicked" and "everything was so natural and easy." My ears perked up as he said this. It's an amazing feeling when things just click with someone and it feels like your souls are connected. But not having to communicate because things are working so well may mean trouble later, because communication is a skill that never gets developed. That is precisely what was happening between Kendall and Sheldon.

Kendall shared he initiated therapy because he and Sheldon had not been intimate in nearly two months. He was feeling rejected and unloved by his partner, and consequently he was "fed up." At this time, Sheldon, who had remained relatively quiet during the session, echoed Kendall and admitted that he was also feeling lonely and rejected.

We discussed their sexual history, unpacking those boxes, which followed the typical patterns I often hear. When they first started dating, they were having sex almost daily. They moved in together after six months and things slowed down drastically, yet they still managed to be intimate once a week. Since moving to a new city two months ago, however, they had not been intimate at all.

It was time for me to do some investigative work and figure out why the most recent change had occurred. Kendall was able to elaborate on a few core details. Since he and Sheldon had moved, they were under a lot of career pressure—particularly Sheldon—whose job had brought them to the area. Kendall confided they had been arguing more frequently, particularly about money, which was atypical for them. Amid all the arguing, their sex life was suffering. More of an observer during the session, Sheldon nodded his head in agreement, echoing Kendall's sentiments once in a while with a "yes" or "no."

When couples argue, it is difficult to feel connected to one another. It can actually make them feel disconnected, unheard, and invalidated, particularly if the issue is not resolved in a timely and appropriate manner. The residual feelings of anger can carry over into the relationship and lead to resentment. Ultimately, it can affect a couple's sex life. Who wants to be vulnerable and intimate with someone from whom they feel disconnected? Or with someone they are angry and resentful towards?

When I pointed this out to Kendall, it resonated. Despite myths that hype the idea of make-up sex, Kendall admitted, "I don't even want to be intimate with Sheldon right now. We argue so much it doesn't feel like *us* anymore." Again, Sheldon nodded in agreement, but did add "but I do want to be intimate."

While we talked more about how the couple argues, it was clear they were not fighting fairly. Kendall frequently got defensive during arguments, then Sheldon would shut down and storm off. Neither would talk for at least several hours and then, rather than readdressing the issue, they would just act like nothing at all had happened. If nothing happened, then nothing was resolved.

The session was nearing to a close and it was time to provide Sheldon and Kendall with some useful tools to implement before our next session. Helping this couple to secure their foundation with better communication was going to help bring intimacy back between them.

I discussed Gottman's theory of the Four Horsemen, as well as ways to be aware of them and how to resolve them when they are used. Gottman refers to this resolution as a "repair." It provides an opportunity to fix one of the Four Horsemen after it has been used within a discussion. It also allows for the discussion to continue, rather than leading to other Horsemen or turning into an argument.

Kendall and Sheldon were both engaging in various forms of The Four Horsemen, and they were able to identify their unhealthy patterns as soon as I explained the concept to them. People usually do not realize that they are exhibiting unhealthy communication patterns, let alone know how to resolve them, until it is pointed out in a reflective manner. Once the problem has been pointed out and is acknowledged by a couple, it becomes much easier to resolve.

Another concept that Gottman identified, one I also see many couples struggling with, is something he refers to as "perpetual gridlock." This is defined as an issue or problem that a couple will always be dealing with, and likely never resolve. Most couples are able to identify at least one issue where they feel they have the same argument over and over again without ever reaching a compromise or resolution. Most times, resolution for a perpetual problem looks like validation.

After I explain the concept of perpetual gridlock to clients, I like to share the following quote from Dan Wile (p. 12):

> ...there is value, when choosing a long-term partner, in realizing that you will inevitably be choosing a particular set of unsolvable problems that you'll be grappling with for the next ten, twenty, or fifty years. The goal of that part of our intervention that deals with problem solving is not to try to get couples to resolve all their problems, but to transform the gridlocked perpetual problems in perpetual problems with which the couple has a dialogue. Less than a third of their problems will have real solutions.

This idea goes along with the concept that we cannot change a person, and we must accept them as they are, faults and all. The only way a person can change is if they want to and they are intrinsically motivated.

Case study: Cindy and Ashton

Cindy and Ashton had been together for just over four years when they came to see me. Cindy was in her mid-20s, finishing up her master's degree in philosophy while bartending on the weekends. Ashton was in his early 30s and worked as a stage-hand at the local community theater. He also occasionally did stand-up comedy around town to supplement the bills. They were open-minded and liberal, funny and laid back. They told me the hilarious story of how they met, after literally running into each other—on two separate occasions. The first time, they awkwardly apologized to each other. The second time, they decided it must be fate. Cindy asked Ashton out on a date. "Who runs into another human being, *twice?!*" Cindy exclaimed. As they retold the story, we all laughed, and I could see the connection this couple had.

After dating for two years, they moved in together. "It seemed like a natural progression to move in together," Ashton admitted. I asked them about their intimate life and Cindy reported they were intimate about twice a week, although Ashton felt it was more like once a week. They both agreed they were satisfied with their sex life. "At least, I thought we had a good sex life, until now…" Cindy mused.

Two weeks ago, Cindy had discovered a box in the corner of Ashton's closet while putting away the laundry. She admitted she had never noticed the box and her curiosity caused her to open it. She discovered it was full of leather and rubber clothing. Cindy said the discovery was both overwhelming and emotional for her. "Honestly, I wasn't sure what to think. So I just put the lid back on and kept putting away the laundry." Unsure how to react to the contents within, she decided to pretend she had never seen the box, let alone opened it. Cindy admitted that her inner thoughts got the best of her, and a week later she confronted Ashton. By the time Cindy talked to Ashton, she said, "I had convinced myself of all kinds of things. I was sure he was cheating on me."

After a long conversation in which Ashton assured Cindy that he was not having an affair, he admitted to having a sexual fetish. He had hidden it from Cindy for many years because he was afraid he would be rejected. Ashton felt like it was also something personal, and was not necessarily something he wanted to experience with Cindy. He felt like he was not hurting himself or anyone else. Cindy felt differently, and they decided to schedule a therapy appointment.

"You've been lying to me all these years," she accused. "Am I just supposed to be okay with this? Just start living out this… this…fantasy with you?"

Ashton explained that he was not asking her to do anything. "For me it's not some kinky sexual fantasy, Cindy. This is part of who I am. Most of the time it's not even sexual." Cindy did not understand. Ashton tried to explain it more in-depth. "I just feel so all over the place all the time. Everything is chaotic. When I was a kid, my dad put me in a leather jacket and took me on his motorcycle. It was during a time when things were especially chaotic at home. The constraints of the leather made me feel safe. I feel safe. And sometimes I find release." While Cindy was beginning to understand where Ashton was coming from, because she was willing to listen to him in a moderated setting, she was still allowing her emotional state to overcome her. "I don't understand why you can't just wear a leather jacket then. Why do you have to…own all these weird clothes?" she questioned through sobs.

It took several sessions for Cindy and Ashton to be able to validate one another and listen to each other's concerns, utilizing exercises from the Kink chapter. However, it quickly became clear that they were at a point of perpetual gridlock. Cindy was never going to understand Ashton's need for wearing leather and rubber. Ashton was never going to understand why Cindy was taking it so personally. Once they were able to become less emotional during this discussion, I helped them to work through and discuss their perpetual gridlock.

I pulled out a whiteboard in my office and facilitated a discussion where they each took turns listing why they were, or were not, okay with Ashton wearing rubber and leather. As they each contributed to the list, I explained that it was okay for them not to understand each other but they did need to validate one another. (For example, I think beets taste terrible so I don't understand wanting to eat them, but I hear those of you who say they taste good and are healthy for you. And I validate your opinion! As long as you validate mine and don't make me eat them. Please!)

Over time, the concept of perpetual gridlock helped them reach a place of mutual respect and compromise.

It was especially useful to unpack their boxes and put their opinions on a whiteboard because it forced both of them to use a variety of communication forms to look, listen, and read what their partner was thinking and experiencing.

Ultimately, Cindy wanted nothing to do with Ashton's fetish. Through therapy and communicating with her partner, she also came to realize that up until now, she *had* nothing to do with Ashton's fetish. This was what allowed her to come from a place of reasoning and healing. In some ways, she gave herself validation.

While Cindy used this realization to humble and heal herself, Ashton was able to admit his own fault in the situation. He admitted that he should have shared this very personal piece of himself with Cindy earlier in their relationship. He still felt strongly that he was not hurting anyone. From a very literal perspective, Cindy was able to agree with this.

Despite reaching a place of validation and listening to one another, they had a difficult time figuring out where to go from there. We spent time brainstorming ideas: good ones, bad ones, and perhaps unrealistic ones.

The couple eventually agreed that Cindy would have a night out twice a month, and Ashton could use this time to wear the contents in his box. Cindy felt like Ashton was not keeping a secret if she knew what he was doing, but she also felt being away from home kept her from being involved. Ashton was thankful to not have to keep this box a secret anymore, and he appreciated the respect Cindy was giving him to have this release. They also agreed to discuss the issue on occasion, even if they reached the same conclusion each and every time. That's the funny thing about perpetual gridlock: the same conclusion may come about every time, but it creates a platform for couples to have a conversation that comes from mutual respect, love, and a sense of validation and understanding.

Communication can be very difficult. We may feel embarrassed, ashamed, and vulnerable to share our innermost thoughts and feelings with someone. But without good communication, problems are inevitable. Like I said earlier, we are all terrible mind-readers.

There are many exercises couples can do to help with communication skills. Work through the following exercises to improve communication within your own relationships.

■ EXERCISE ■

Review Gottman's Four Horsemen: *criticism, stonewalling, contempt,* and *defensiveness.* Which ones are you guilty of doing? Your partner? Discuss and share. How will you be mindful of your own communication skills in order to improve communication with your partner?

■ EXERCISE ■

Couples often say they have nothing to talk about anymore. They think they know everything about one another. The conversations are transactional, if anything, meaning couples talk about what is for dinner, who will drive the kids to soccer practice, if the phone bill was paid this month, and other mundane things. It's not to say these are not important things to communicate, but the communication is done to complete tasks and check things off of lists. It is not done in a way that creates intimacy, builds trust, or solidifies the foundation of the relationship.

Couples can work through the following questions to start doing these things. You can answer the questions together, or do them separately and then talk about them later. Do not rush through the questions. Pick a few to answer at a time. Remember, you do not have to like what your partner says, or agree with them. This is an opportunity to unpack boxes and create new ones. You do need to trust that your partner is answering honestly, being vulnerable, and communicating with you. I shared an example from my own memory for the first two questions to illustrate the intention of the exercise.

1. Favorite color? Why? For example: *I remember being at an Easter egg hunt when I was about three years old. My favorite color was pink and I was adamant that I only pick up the pink eggs. I started getting a lot more eggs in my basket when blue became my second favorite color.*

2. Discuss one of your favorite childhood memories. Describe the memory and try to remember what it felt like, tasted like, smelled like, and looked like. For example: *I went skiing for the first time when I was seven. It felt scary and nerve-wracking. It tasted like bitter cold air in winter. It smelled like stinky feet in the lodge where people put their ski boots on/off. It looked white as snow. It is also a fond memory, when I learned to pizza-wedge, spend time with my dad, and learned the only sport I've ever enjoyed.*

3. If you get to choose what is for dinner, what would you eat, and why?

4. When you're angry, what do you need from your partner?

5. When you're upset or sad, what do you need from your partner?

6. What motivates you?

7. What makes you feel most vulnerable? Or when do you feel most vulnerable?

8. What is your favorite shirt? Why? How do you feel when you wear it?

9. Discuss a time when you lost someone. How did it feel then? How does it feel now?

10. What is your greatest accomplishment? Why?

11. What first attracted you to your partner?

12. What makes you feel sexy?

13. What turns you on? What turns you off?

14. How would you define sex? Sexuality? How do these words make you feel?

15. Have you ever been in a situation where you did not give consent for something to happen? How did you handle the situation? How did it make you feel? Your example does not have to be sexually related.

16. If you had to describe your sexual self in the form of an object, what would it be? Why?

17. How would you describe flirting? Discuss a time when you and your partner flirted.

18. Have/would you ever use a sex toy? For example: a vibrator, dildo, anal beads, restraints, blindfolds.

19. Why do you choose to look at, or abstain from, pornography? Does your answer change if you were to look at it with your current partner? Discuss how this makes you feel.

20. What motivates you to masturbate?

21. How does hugging your partner make you feel?

22. Would you prefer sex on the beach or in the forest?

23. Describe a sexual fantasy you have. It does not have to be one you want to experience in real life. See the Fantasy chapter if you are struggling to answer this.

24. What is your favorite body part on yourself? What is your favorite body part on your partner?

25. What is a quality or characteristic about your partner that you admire?

26. What cartoon character do you find sexy?

27. Do you think it is harder to talk about sex, or to initiate and have sex?

28. What time of day do you prefer to have sex?

29. Who taught you about sex growing up? Did you receive any kind of formal sex education?

30. When was the first time you watched pornography? How did it make you feel? How do you feel about pornography now?

31. How would you describe your sexual self?

32. Sex on the beach or slushies?

33. Do you think there is a difference between making love and having sex? Why or why not?

34. If you had to describe your sex life by the title of a movie, which film would it be?

35. Where do you dislike being touched?

36. Discuss a time when you had a same-sex attraction.

37. What did you call your genitals as a child? What do you call them now? How do you refer to them when being intimate? What do you call your partner's genitals?

38. If you had to play a musical album on repeat every time you were intimate, what would you choose and why?

39. Which of your five senses makes you want to be intimate? Hearing? Tasting? Touching? Seeing? Smelling? Which do you end up using the most during intimacy?

40. How old were you the first time you masturbated? How did it make you feel? How do you feel about masturbation now?

41. How do you like to be shown love? How do you express loving feelings to your partner?

42. How do you feel about sex during menstruation?

43. Write sexy haiku (5 syllables) Make it erotic and fun (7 syllables) Then share your poem (5 syllables)

44. If there was one thing about sex you wish your parents would've talked to you about growing up, what would it be?

45. In what situation are you most likely to have an affair? Where are you and with whom?

46. Would you ever consider an open relationship? Why? (An open relationship is when you and your partner give each other permission to have casual sex with other people. You may or may not discuss your experiences. Typically the interaction is purely for physical enjoyment and is not emotionally charged. You can read more about this in the chapter *Polyamory, Open Relationships, and Swinging.*)

47. Would you ever consider a polyamorous relationship? Why? (Polyamory is when you and your partner agree to date others. It is different than an open relationship because it is based on having an emotional connection with another person (other than your partner), which may then become sexual, but is not casual. Typically there is a commitment to your partner and at least one other person. You can read more about this in the chapter *Polyamory, Open Relationships, and Swinging.*)

48. Would you ever engage in swinging or swapping partners? Why? (This is when you and your partner engage in sex with another couple together. You can read more about this in *Polyamory, Open Relationships, and Swinging.*)

49. What motivates you to have sex? What keeps you from having more sex?

50. What prompted you to read this book?

51. What are your strengths as a couple?

52. Lights on or off during intimacy? Why?

53. How do you feel about your relationship today?

VULNERABILITY

If you want to improve yourself and your relationship, you have to allow yourself to be vulnerable. At the end of the day, when you remove all of the materialistic comforts from your life, all you have left is human connection. If you squander those opportunities to connect with others, you may not have anything of value left. However, we are raised in an individualistic society where we are taught to be leaders and strive for success. The idea of being someone who has accomplished something equates to being wealthy.

Children are often told to "buck up," to "stop being such a girl," or called a "crybaby." This is particularly aimed at young boys who are encouraged to suppress their emotions or risk being seen as "weak." Feelings are reserved for girls who are "emotional" and "drama queens." There is a stereotype that equates showing emotions with being weak, and we are taught you won't achieve anything in our society if you are weak. However, you won't achieve anything in life if you shut everyone out either. As nice as it is to have, money doesn't buy happiness. Vulnerability, which leads to human and emotional connection, just might.

English-Irish poet David Whyte speaks at length about the emotional state of vulnerability. He acknowledges its complexities, but also recognizes vulnerability as a natural phenomenon we all experience and encounter. It is whether we choose to allow ourselves to experience that natural emotional state, or abandon our natural state of emotion. Whyte elaborates wildly, noting that:

> *Vulnerability is not a weakness, a passing indisposition, or something we can arrange to do without, vulnerability is not a choice, vulnerability is the underlying, ever present and abiding undercurrent of our natural state. To run from vulnerability is to run from the essence of our nature, the attempt to be invulnerable is the vain attempt to become something we are not and most especially, to close off our understanding of the grief of others. More seriously, in refusing our vulnerability we refuse the help needed at every turn of our existence and immobilize the essential, tidal and conversational foundations of our identity.*

> *To have a temporary, isolated sense of power over all events and circumstances, is a lovely illusionary privilege and perhaps the prime and most beautifully constructed conceit of being human and especially of being youthfully human, but it is a privilege that must be surrendered with that same youth, with ill health, with accident, with the loss of loved ones who do not share our untouchable powers; powers eventually and most emphatically given up, as we approach our last breath.*

> *The only choice we have as we mature is how we inhabit our vulnerability, how we become larger and*

more courageous and more compassionate through our
intimacy with disappearance, our choice is to inhabit
vulnerability as generous citizens of loss, robustly
and fully, or conversely, as misers and complainers,
reluctant and fearful, always at the gates of existence,
but never bravely and completely attempting to enter,
never wanting to risk ourselves, never walking fully
through the door.

Whyte affirms the natural existence of vulnerability while also acknowledging the selfishness of existence when we refuse to experience it. At its core, the refusal to be vulnerable prohibits us from being genuine and keeps everyone at bay. Its refusal is rooted in control issues, but then leaves us deeply wounded at times when vulnerability is unavoidable, such as losing a relationship, a loved one, or experiencing one's own mortality. Whyte notes that the act of choosing to *not* be vulnerable speaks to being vain, privileged, and youthful. While I would agree, I would challenge that a life without vulnerability isn't much of a privilege at all since it is rooted in isolation.

A box I like to open and share with clients about vulnerability is one of my own. To offer some backstory: my parents divorced when I was ten years old, and I lived in a different state than my father. When I was about 12, my father remarried and his wife shared a story with me about vulnerability. It was a story about putting yourself out there, saying the things you feel, and not living with regret. At the time, the story opened a gateway to connect with my father. Due to the distance, we spent a lot of time talking on the phone, and this invitation to express myself fostered our relationship. Over 20 years later we end every phone call with, "I love you and miss you."

This was really difficult for my father initially. He grew up in a household where hugs and "I love you's" were non-existent.

In fact, I remember the first time his mother (my grandmother) said she loved me. I literally didn't know what to say and I froze in place. Rather than reciprocating, I choked out a questioning response, "I love you too?" It was the only time I can recall her expressing her love for me.

This got me thinking about my grandfather, her husband. They grew up during World War II, my grandmother a German native and my grandfather raised by his mother, a single and fiercely independent woman, a feminist role model, and a product of the Great Depression. Feelings were a luxury, food and stability were a necessity. My great-grandmother lived until she was 103, wearing high heels and sporting a trendy sweater until her passing. When people you love begin to pass, it makes you think about mortality.I had lived many years never expressing my affection for my grandfather. His way of showing love was to slip me $50 after I flew out for a visit.

A few years ago, I recalled the lesson my stepmother had instilled from childhood. I didn't want my grandfather to pass away without ever having told him that I *do* love him. He is a stubborn old man who lacks empathy but has a great sense of humor and energy. One day, we were talking on the phone, as we do on occasion, and a stint of bravery swept over me just before we ended our conversation. "I love you," I spit out, and my grandfather hung up on me. I had made myself vulnerable, told him I care about him, and the old man hung up on me. I was taken aback but also proud of myself. Next time we talked on the phone, I did it again. "I love you." I heard a grumble from 1,500 miles away and he mumbled, "you too," then abruptly hung up the phone. I kept at it and over the years, he eventually reciprocated those words. This is a love my grandfather had never been given permission to express, but with patience and time he gave himself permission to express it to me.

Recently, I was talking to him on the phone after sending him chocolates. He was informing me that I couldn't afford to be buying him chocolate so he sent me a check to pay me back, confirming money is still his way of expressing his feelings. Before we ended the conversation he said, "I love you" before I got a chance to. I reciprocated, hung up the phone, and cried. Nearly five years later, my grandfather had said he loved me first. It has been one of the most valuable experiences in my life, and I am grateful I had the opportunity to be vulnerable with this man.

The story of my grandfather is my favorite story of vulnerability to share because it sets the tone for how difficult it can be to share our feelings given the environment we are raised in, but it also highlights the payoff of creating new boxes.

Most people coming to sex therapy aren't seeking advice on how to open up to their grandfather, *but* the story does set the stage for putting yourself out there, taking a risk, not knowing the reaction you will receive. It is also an example of communication and an illustration of making yourself vulnerable. My story has resonated with people who are in a situation where they are scared to open up to their partner about something, whether that be telling them about a fantasy they are craving, a fetish they engage in, or something else deeply personal. When we feel ashamed, embarrassed, or scared that someone we care about will judge us, we tend to feel that keeping a secret outweighs the risk of vulnerability. And while it may protect you from judgment or embarrassment, it also prevents you from being your authentic self.

Case study: Goutam

One young man came to see me after allowing himself to be vulnerable, and he was unsure how to move forward. Goutam was a 25-year-old male who moved to the United States two years ago after finishing university in Bangladesh. He grew up as an only child in a middle-class Muslim family. After university, Goutam decided to focus on achieving financial success. His parents supported his endeavors and did not pressure him into an arranged marriage. In his home city, he was working successfully in IT and was beginning to enjoy financial stability when he decided to pursue an opportunity to live abroad. Goutam didn't know anyone when he arrived in the United States, but was able to arrange for a roommate, an acquaintance from India named Abdul.

Being a self-described introvert, Goutam had not made a lot of friends outside of his roommate or co-workers over the two years. He said that he enjoyed hanging out with his co-workers on occasion, but did not enjoy American bar culture as much as they seemed to. So, he ended up spending a lot of his time at home with his roommate Abdul.

Over the course of their first year living together, Goutam began to develop an emotional attachment to Abdul, and slowly realized he was falling in love with him. The feelings brought about anxiety and confusion for Goutam. He questioned his instincts. He questioned his attraction. He questioned his religion. And he questioned himself. Goutam began to realize that historically he had only developed feelings for another person after a deep emotional connection had transpired. He wasn't sure what this meant for his sexual orientation.

For a year, Goutam kept his feelings a secret from Abdul as he battled his own feelings of humiliation, shame, guilt, and fear. Slowly, he began to accept that he had fallen in love with Abdul. One day, Goutam decided to confide his truth and tell Abdul how he felt. Abdul rejected him and their friendship almost dissolved. The idea of homosexuality was not acceptable in Bangladesh or India, and Abdul was not only put-off by the entire idea, he was offended.

Goutam was heartbroken and unsure how to move forward. He had no support system or other friends, and he was overwhelmed with anxiety during his daily encounters with Abdul as they continued to live together. Goutam had done his best to ignore the emotional connection he felt to Abdul, but upon learning that Abdul would be entering into an arranged marriage over the summer, Goutam was crushed. His anxiety spiraled out of control. Goutam was beside himself and unsure how to move forward, without Abdul by his side. He shared his heartbreaking truth with a sense of exposure that few possess.

While the reality of Goutam's situation was poignant, it was also one of the most exemplary stories of vulnerability I have ever heard. I think we can all learn a lot about being true to ourselves from Goutam. Part of the work Goutam did in therapy was to practice remaining open to others, as his inclination after being rejected by Abdul was to shut down and swear off love. His dedication to himself, as shown by his investment in therapy, was what we capitalized on to maintain an incentive to work on having continued self-introspection and the ability to speak his truth.

About a year into therapy, Goutam had begun to believe in himself again. His anxiety was now manageable and he had moved into an apartment by himself. In an effort to make new friends and combat his introversion, he joined a local hiking club. He started to make local friends and even asked a woman out on a date. Before we terminated therapy, Goutam expressed he was cautiously optimistic and trying to allow himself to be free to have emotional connections with others. I hope that we can all find the emotional capacity Goutam displayed as we find the power to express our own emotional vulnerabilities.

■ EXERCISE ■

Allowing yourself to create a new box full of vulnerability takes time, practice, and patience. If it is something you have not done before, there is no better time to start than right now.

The first part of this exercise should be done alone. If you allow yourself to be vulnerable with someone else, you have to first let yourself engage in self-awareness regarding your own thoughts, feelings, and emotions. Start by finding time when you can be by yourself, uninterrupted. Make sure you feel calm and are free from distractions. Turn your phone off, play some music, light a candle, and take a deep breath to get started. Once you feel relaxed, consider the following questions. You may choose to record them in a journal, simply think them through, or discuss them with a therapist.

1. When was the first time you told someone you loved them? Who was it? How did it make you feel?

2. How do you feel abut your gender? Do you like being a man or a woman? When did you first have an aware-ness of your gender? How often do you think about your gender? How does your gender impact you on a daily basis?

3. When was the first time you experienced same-sex attrac-tion? How did it make you feel? Did you ever tell anyone? Did you ever act on it?

4. When was the first time you felt shame? How old were you? What happened? Did thinking about the memory bring up the same feelings of shame?

5. How do you feel about your genitals? If you feel comfort-able pushing yourself, take your clothes off. Stand in front of a mirror and look at your genitals. Does this change

how you feel about them? Are you met with feelings of curiosity? Admiration? Shame? Embarrassment?

6. Have you ever faked an orgasm to prevent yourself from being vulnerable? With who? Why? How did it make you feel?

7. What makes you feel vulnerable? If the previous questions were easy to answer, consider what other questions would make you feel particularly vulnerable.

■ **EXERCISE** ■

On a separate occasion, you and your partner should find time when you will be free from any distractions. Choose a place where you can relax and feel safe. While the bedroom can be a place to engage in a conversation that feels romantic, I would encourage you to choose a more neutral setting such as sitting on the floor in your living room or at the kitchen table. Set some ground rules so you both feel relaxed. For example, engage in active listening, be open-minded, trust, and be open (after all this is about being vulnerable). Put your phone away and remove any other distractions from your immediate surroundings. You may choose to play some music or light candles. Once you feel relaxed, take turns answering the following questions:

1. In what situation are you most likely to cheat on the person sitting across from you? Bear in mind, answering this question does not indicate that you or your partner has had an affair, or will have one. What it does mean is that you are giving forethought to a situation, which becomes more easily avoided when acknowledged and thought through. How can you support each other so neither of you ends up in this situation? What could you

do to support each other in this situation, prior to making a choice you regret?

2. Have you ever lied to the person sitting in front of you? What was it about? Why did you do it?

3. Discuss a fantasy that you would like to engage in with the person sitting across from you. It does *not* have to be a sexual fantasy.

4. What makes you feel most insecure about yourself? Is it a part of your body? Your financial status? Your childhood? After you've discussed what makes you feel insecure about yourself, share what you are most insecure about in the relationship. Note, this doesn't mean one of you is leaving the relationship. This is about sharing your vulnerabilities and truth. Breathe, do not judge, and be open.

5. What is hardest for you to communicate with your partner? Why?

6. How do you feel about pornography? Do you enjoy watching it? Why or why not? Where did your beliefs about pornography develop?

Once you have both answered all of the above questions, talk about how this experience was for each of you. Was it difficult? Do you feel better? Worse? Why? Be sure to express thanks and gratitude to your partner for listening and sharing.

LOW LIBIDO

Nearly 40 million women suffer from low libido in the United States. Many of them never make it to my office. The women that do often have similar stories. More often than not, these women will share that their sex life started out exciting. Even if it wasn't, women can usually attest that they had more sex with their partner when they first started dating than they do now. If they are self-motivated to come to therapy, it is because they know they deserve to be sexually satisfied and feel they are missing out on something due to their lack of desire.

While the history of a couple's sex life is important, so is their current routine. The next question then is, how often does the couple have sex now? This question is really important since it sheds light on the current factors in a couple's relationship and follows with a discussion about libido, arousal, and desire.

I find it interesting that women, and sometimes men, come into my office proclaiming they have low libido. "How do you know it's low?" I typically challenge. Some couples, who used to have sex daily when they first started dating, and now only have sex once a week, think their libido has decreased. Other couples that had sex once a week when they started dating, and now have sex four times a year, are quite satisfied with their sex life.

So who defines low libido? What is libido? According to the *Merriam-Webster Dictionary,* libido is defined as "sexual drive." In order to have a libido, a person must also have a desire to be intimate. Desire, as defined by *Merriam-Webster,* is "to want or wish for." Women typically need to have desire before they feel arousal, which then increases libido. In contrast, men typically feel aroused first, which increases libido and then creates desire. Arousal, a verb, is by defined by *Merriam-Webster* as, "to excite" or "to rouse or stimulate to action or to physiological readiness for activity."

Libido does not exist without desire and arousal, but desire and arousal cannot be created without intimate experiences. So when a person avoids intimate experiences, they also eliminate their libido. In some ways that old saying is accurate: "if you don't use it, you lose it." Passion and desire among most couples fizzles within two years, and for many, it does not extend beyond six months.

Many people label themselves as having low libido, and most self-diagnose. Others come to therapy feeling completely content if they never had sex again, but their partner pushes them to engage in therapy. If a person does not feel there is a problem, it is difficult to address in therapy.

There are many factors that can contribute to low libido. This is where therapy can get convoluted, especially if there is more than one reason at hand. Sexual trauma, pregnancy, birth, children, cancer, marriage, divorce, medications, death of a loved one, loss of attraction, body dysmorphia, boredom, an unhealthy relationship, work, laundry, dishes, and exhaustion can all contribute to low libido. When these issues are coupled with other issues, it can be necessary for a sex therapist to get involved in helping to resolve issues, rather than trying to tackle them alone. Can you identify with any of these reasons that may contribute to your own low libido?

It is also important to normalize the fact that sometimes a person just isn't in the mood to engage in intimacy or have sex. Does this mean they have low libido? Not necessarily. It is valid for a person to be exhausted after working eight hours and then making dinner and putting the kids to bed. If a woman feels comfortable in her relationship, and her partner respects her boundaries, than it is okay to be too tired to have sex. But it's a problem when saying "no" becomes an automatic response every time your partner initiates intimacy. At some point, the reasons become excuses, which can lead to issues.

Interestingly, clients who come to therapy for an hour a week may also say they do not have time to be intimate. I would challenge that if they can find an hour a week for therapy, they can find an hour a week to be intimate with their partner. That being said, being intimate does not necessarily mean having intercourse. I encourage couples to just prioritize spending adult time together. During this time, they are not allowed to talk about work, kids, or money.

Sadly, many couples find they do not have a lot in common when these topics are removed from their discussions. However, it does create a unique opportunity for them to reconnect. Many people lose themselves in the daily grind and forget about the things that matter, like being intimate with their partner. The talking exercise at the end of the *Communication* chapter is a useful starting point.

Case study: Brier and Scott

"I never want to have sex again," said Brier, a young woman in her late 20s who had been married just over a year. "It's nothing against Scott," she said, defending her partner. "He's smart, he works hard, and I find him attractive. When we first started dating we had a great sex life. But now, I'm just not interested."

Brier's story sounds like many women's. Brier worked as a pediatric nurse who was scheduled for 12-hour shifts. When she gets home, "I just want to relax and unwind. The last thing I want to do is have sex. When we do, it's fine, but I want him to hurry up so it's over." For Brier, she was overworked and tired and wanted to relax in her free time. Sex felt like the opposite for her. The pressure of being intimate after working a 12-hour day was overwhelming. When Scott would initiate, and she agreed to be intimate, she was busy thinking about how messy their house was or her to-do list so she was not focused on the physicality occurring between them.

Case study: Aimee and Quinn

Another woman, Aimee, came to see me for low libido in her marriage to her husband, Quinn. Intimacy between them had been great while they were dating. After they moved in together and got married, things halted rapidly. This is a frequent occurrence. Weekend flings with a lover quickly become taking out the trash, paying the utility bills, and other stories of unsexy routines. Aimee thought the daily routine and planning a wedding were her reasons for her anxiety and low libido. A few months after they married, Aimee began to feel anxiety anytime Quinn touched her. She began to have flashbacks of being sexually assaulted when she was in college. As she realized what was happening and why she was pushing him away, she felt "guilty for punishing" her husband. She saw Quinn as "gentle, patient, and kind," so this association was particularly confusing for her.

Aimee desperately wanted to resolve this issue and decided to initiate sex therapy. At the end of our first session, she expressed how relieved she felt. "I had been putting off making this appointment because I thought you were going to tell us to just go home and have sex." This is something I hear frequently from first-time clients with low libido, no matter the contributing factors. I recognize libido has been put in a box high on a shelf and I never tell a client to go home and have sex. If it were as simple as "just have sex" then there would not be a problem in the first place. It is also essential not to place pressure, stress, or blame on someone experiencing low libido, as most people tend to put the pressure on themselves.

Although met with a great amount of stigma, plenty of men also experience low libido. Men that come to therapy for low libido often place an unreasonable amount of pressure on themselves. They feel like something is wrong with them for not wanting to have sex with their partner. Their partner may question if he is still attracted to them or is having an affair. In heterosexual relationships, women may or even question if her partner might be gay. Having a lower sex drive is not a sufficient reason to suspect any of these things, but men are "supposed" to be ready to have sex at the drop of a hat. So naturally, his partner assumes the worst. It is likely that, due to the guilt placed on him, he begins to avoid sex altogether and questions if there really is something wrong with him.

Hollywood and pornography portray men as overtly sexual. The male protagonist, always tall, dark, and handsome, is expected to have an instantaneous erection whenever the female protagonist, beautiful, busty, and blonde, walks into a room as the movie progresses to the inevitable sex scene. He is always ready to go. Never a minute to waste as he sweeps her off her feet. A man like this never loses his erection during foreplay, and probably doesn't need foreplay to obtain an erection. He would never tell her he is too tired or stressed out. The man is always ready for sex. So if men aren't like Hollywood actors, then something must be wrong with them. Right? Maybe. Maybe not. As we learned from Brier and Aimee, libido is much more complex than wanting to just have sex at the drop of a hat—or in this case, panties.

So how do I approach the topic of low libido during the first session? It certainly requires active listening and validation. Normalizing where someone is coming from is required. Telling the man who is vulnerable enough to come to therapy that there actually is something wrong with him because he doesn't meet Hollywood standards would be damaging and inaccurate. Not wanting sex all the time doesn't mean a man isn't normal. There is always more inside the box. The first session begins to pull out the contents of the box.

After evaluating a client's comfort level with therapy, with themselves, with their partner, and with discussing sexuality, I may assign them a simple touching exercise. A person who is experiencing low libido is not likely to go home and have sex with their partner, because something is preventing them from wanting to do so in the first place. In fact, more often than not, the first assignment for the couple is to *not have sex,* which can alleviate pressure for them both. The goals for low libido, regardless of the contributing factors, include feeling comfortable with touch, which in turn creates the arousal and desire needed to be comfortable initiating intimacy. You can utilize the exercises that follow to begin finding your own arousal and desire as you again become more comfortable with touch. Also see the exercise at the end of the *Kink* chapter. However, for some couples, even a touching exercise can feel too intimate. If you are one of those people, it is best to start with the questions at the end of the *Communication* chapter.

▪ EXERCISE ▪

In this exercise, the person with low libido is encouraged to initiate a hug with their partner. This is adopted from Dr. David Schnarch's hugging-till-relaxed exercise in his book *Passionate Marriage*. In this exercise, you will have an opportunity to practice intentional initiation of physical touch. You are only encouraged to initiate when you feel comfortable and motivated. It is not to say that as a couple you cannot hug one another at all unless you initiate, but this hug is meant to be intentional and last longer.

After initiating the hug, you should continue to hug for as long as you both feel comfortable. At face value, this exercise may sound silly, but a truly intentional hug can quickly become uncomfortable emotionally or physically. For many, this warm embrace can feel very vulnerable and therefore this could be an ongoing exercise.

After engaging in a hug, consider the following questions:

1. How did it feel initiating the hug?
2. How long did you hug? How did it feel?
3. What were you thinking about during the hug? Who broke contact first? Why?

Once you feel you have mastered this exercise, consider reading *Passionate Marriage* in its entirety. It offers additional context and reasoning for this exercise. Please note that for some couples the exercise feels more intentional after reading Dr. Schnarch's book because they find the exercise has more context and purpose.

I challenge you to consider all of the things hugging can elicit. Why do you hug anyone, ever? Does the intensity of your hugs differ based on who you are hugging?

If after reading this exercise, you feel you are unable to execute it, consider what is most difficult for you and talk to your partner about this.

▪ EXERCISE ▪

Sensate Focus was created by Masters and Johnson in the 1960s for the purpose of connecting through non-demand touch, which in turn creates pleasurable intimacy and emotional connection. There are many variations of this exercise. In the version I use, the first step is a facial touching exercise. As a couple, you will take turns touching one another's face. Not only can this exercise be connecting as you look into your partner's eyes, it can also feel extremely vulnerable. Ideally this exercise is done for a total of 40–60 minutes, with each person taking a turn to touch the other's face. However, depending on your own comfort levels, I encourage you to do the exercise for as long as you see fit. Some people are only able to spend three minutes having their face touched before they need to end the exercise. The goal then is to elongate the time as you become more comfortable with it.

Before you begin this exercise, make sure you and your partner have found a comfortable and private space. You do not want to be interrupted by your children, the phone ringing, or the kitchen timer going off. Some people like to make the setting more romantic by lighting candles or filling up a warm bath.

You will want to set aside enough time so that each of you can do the exercise and reciprocate it. Perhaps you'd like to just do it for three minutes the first time, and then have your partner reciprocate for three minutes. If you feel more comfortable, you can do each step for 20–30 minutes each. Limit talking during the implementation of the exercises, but do discuss the process afterwards. Try a variation of pressure and touch while doing Sensate Focus. Practice being present in your own mind and body.

Step One: Facial Touching You may like to remove your clothing during this exercise, or you may feel more comfortable with your clothing on. Clothes are actually irrelevant to Step One except for hats—you'll need to remove that. As noted, this is a facial exercise, which means all of the touching occurs from the neck up. Take your time touching your partner's neck, face, and head. Make sure you touch behind the ears. Caress the eyebrows. Gently rub your partner's lips with your fingertips. Provide a light head massage. Look into your partner's eyes. Gaze into their soul. Find yourself connecting on a whole new intimate level. Switch.

Step Two: Clothed Body Touching During this step, each partner should remain fully clothed. Take turns touching one another from head to toe. You may choose to repeat some of Step One. Make sure you touch your partner behind the knees. Massage their back. Lightly touch their arms. While this exercise is best done laying down, encourage your partner to roll over at some point so you are able to touch their entire body. This portion of the exercise should *not* include touching the genitals or buttocks. Switch.

Step Three: Naked Body Touching Before starting Step Three, you and your partner should feel *very* comfortable executing steps One and Two. If one of you is not, then you should continue to do steps One and Two. Once you are ready for Step Three, both of you should undress. You may choose to undress one another as part of the process, or undress in front of one another. If one of you is experiencing some discomfort with a certain portion of the body (example, breasts, or stomach) due to body image issues, you may choose to modify this step so that portion of the body is covered. Since step three does not involve genital touching, undergarments may be kept on, but you can certainly be fully naked and just not engage in genital touching. Proceed to touch your partner's body. Gently caress their thighs. Lightly touch their stomach and chest. Make sure to touch and caress your partner's head, just as in Step One.

Step Four: Genital Touching Step Four should not be done until each partner feels totally comfortable implementing steps One through Three. Once couples are ready to execute step Four, they should repeat steps One through Three as well. Couples should be undressed for this step. They should take gentle care to touch their partner's genitals, and to ask questions about their comfort level as they go. The goal of this step is not to initiate sex (oral, anal, or vaginal) even if both partners become aroused, especially the first time this step is done. This holds true even if a male partner is struggling with erectile dysfunction and obtains an erection.

Once both partners become reasonably comfortable doing steps One through Four, Sensate Focus exercises can be used as a reset for connection. It should continue to be used as an exercise to build closeness, recreate intimacy and desire, and foster discussion and communication. Sensate Focus is a great exercise for couples seeking to reconnect. It can be done as often as needed. It encourages couples to prioritize one another and take their time as they get to know one another all over again. It is also a spiritually connecting experience for many as they idolize their partner's embodiment.

SEXUAL SCRIPTS

A sexual script is described as "a label that captures the blend of thoughts (beliefs, assumptions, perceptions, attributions, and expectations) that encompass the meaning of the issue and the way in which to handle it" (McCarthy, 2010, p. 42). In other words, sexual scripts are the boxes we fill with messages we have received about sex, and how we accept and personalize those messages. In their book, *Enduring Desire*, Barry McCarthy and Michael Metz speak at length about the concept of sexual scripts and the sexual routines couples engage in. Sexual scripts may include the time couples choose to have sex (morning, for example), the frequency (for example, once a week), who initiates (ex., always him), how sex is initiated (ex., placing her hand on his erect penis), and the intimate acts they engage in (ex., sexual intercourse with woman on top). Oftentimes couples have the same sexual script for long periods of time. For some couples, having a script to abide by is effective. They each know what to expect and when. However, many other couples find themselves bored with their sex lives. This feeling of dissatisfaction can lead to a decrease in sexual frequency and may also lead to one partner having an affair. It is essential for most couples to rewrite their sexual scripts every so often.

After explaining the concept of sexual scripts, I encourage couples to have a discussion about the sexual script that society has written for monogamous couples. I want them to take a critical look at how outside influences have impacted their intimate relationship. Movies, books, television, and pornography show a different viewpoint of sexuality. It is often an unrealistic one that involves edits, cuts, and do-overs. It is a Hollywood script, not a sexual script, and it involves little, if any, communication, a lack of intimacy and love, and almost always has a goal of having an orgasm. In Hollywood and pornography it seems everyone achieves this goal. The real life pressure to perform and have an orgasm can cause anxiety, which can result in sexual issues such as the ones discussed in this book.

Due to the goal of orgasm, people forget the rest of the journey: flirting, foreplay, closeness, stress release, and intimacy. The playfulness is removed and soon forgotten, to a point where it becomes awkward to figure out how to recreate it. On average, it takes women about 20 minutes to become aroused. When a woman feels rushed to engage in penetrative sex or feels like she is taking *too* long to become aroused, she often foregoes the urge to orgasm. This can make it more difficult for her partner to orgasm too—and both are left disappointed. This completely undermines the entire sexual experience and is the start of a disappointing sexual script that may occur again and again until the couple decides it is no longer worth engaging in the script at all. For those couples, they should go back and read the chapter on *Low Libido*. Hopefully, couples can recognize when their sexual script needs to be rewritten, and boxes recycled, before it gets to this point.

Case study: Elliot and Genevieve

My client Elliot, a 56-year-old heterosexual man, complained that he and his wife had been engaging in the same sexual script for 20 years. We discussed their sexual history, and Elliot recalled when they were dating and their sexual relationship could be described as "wild and free." He said, "Genevieve was always willing to experiment when we were dating. We got married two years later and got pregnant right away. The most wild thing that happens anymore is ordering pizza on Saturday nights, with extra cheese!" Elliot was bored with the sexual script he and Genevieve had written for themselves so he decided to initiate therapy.

I wanted to get some more background information on this couple's sex life to determine what had changed over the years and to get a better idea of what their sexual script looked like now. The couple shared that, while they were raising their children, they would have sex one or two times per month, but only after the kids went to bed, only in their bedroom, only with the lights out, and only in the missionary position. Neither described themselves as particularly conservative, but when it came to sex, that is what had transpired. Sex was about being as quiet as possible and doing it as quickly as possible so they would not wake their children. This method quickly became a routine. Genevieve admitted to getting little satisfaction out of it but felt obligated to connect to her husband and allow him a sexual release. She had become so accustomed to this routine that she lost her sense of being a sexual being. Sex was merely part of her "wifely duties."

Elliot was thankful that Genevieve put his needs before her own, but was also sad that she had not been enjoying herself. He regretted they had not discussed their sex life until very recently and had fallen into such an apathetic routine.

Elliot and Genevieve's children were all grown up now. Without them tucked away in their beds, it became blatantly clear their sexual script needed to change. Genevieve quickly identified with the concept of a sexual script. "I hadn't thought of it that way, Kristen, but that's exactly what we do! It's like we've been rehearsing the same play for 18 years. And the show always ends the same." Genevieve and Elliot were so out of touch intimately they did not know how to get back on track. Luckily, they were both motivated to reconnect and prioritize their relationship. At their core they still loved each other and enjoyed spending time together.

So how does one change the boxes they have stored, and rewrite a sexual script? It should start with communication. Both Elliot and Genevieve were unsatisfied with their sexual script, but it had become such a part of their routine that neither thought to talk about it. "Even if we had thought of it, how could I have brought it up?" Genevieve admitted during our session. Obviously, it was brought up eventually, as they found themselves in my office. Genevieve, in particular, had become accustomed to this routine. She developed a fear that bringing up her own frustrations would push Elliot away—or worse, that the sexual script would change in a negative way and sex would suddenly be more than just routine, that it might become painful or last longer. Genevieve couldn't bear the thought of their sex life getting any worse, or of losing her partner. So she continued to follow the script and put Elliot's needs before her own, for 20 years.

Elliot had sensed that Genevieve was not satisfied with their sexual interactions, but he had no idea she was reaching the point of resenting them altogether. He assumed his wife just had difficulty having an orgasm and sensed her hesitation to engage. Elliot also feared that if he said something, their sex life might become non-existent, so he thought it was safer to just continue the script.

Part of rewriting the sexual script is the exploration and development of the relationship in other ways. I told Elliot and

Genevieve to take some time off from having intercourse and to allow themselves the time to rewrite the script. The couple agreed they would not have intercourse for the next eight weeks and would spend this time continuing therapy and learning to connect in other ways.

I encourage clients to find common interests and have discussions that have not been a part of their script. Genevieve and Elliot started with taking their dogs to the dog park. It was an activity they thought they would both enjoy and it allowed them an opportunity to interact. The dog park quickly became an outlet that allowed the playfulness in each of them to naturally come out, ultimately letting their guards down and becoming flirtatious again. As couples get to know each other in new ways, this playfulness occurs and allows eroticism to grow.

In addition to finding common activities together, couples are encouraged to have conversations together. Many couples fall into such a life script that their discussions revolve around work, finances, and their children. When these topics are off limits, many people suddenly find themselves at a loss of what to talk about. Even couples who have poor sex lives but proclaim they are best friends often find they are barely connected once these topics are off limits. Couples should set aside "adult time" each week to talk about anything else: the latest news story, a book they are reading, what they feel passionate about, or where they want to travel. Connecting about daily life can then encourage the discussion about their sexual script. Practicing discussing other topics also makes addressing the sexual script easier.

Couples are also encouraged to discuss fantasies, their likes and dislikes, and even reminisce about the best sex they've had together. Discussing fantasies, even if they are never played out, allows a couple to be more honest and playful with one another. This is discussed further in the chapter on *Fantasy*.

If sex is not occurring, or it has become a routine you can't stand anymore, start by not having sex for a few weeks, like Elliot and Genevieve did. Find 30 minutes a day to connect. Follow the prescribed method: you are not allowed to talk about finances, kids, housework, or careers. If you are stuck, look up a current news article. Perhaps discuss a future trip you'd like to plan. See the questions from the *Communication* chapter to help create additional dialogue.

Once you become more comfortable engaging in conversations, start discussing and addressing your sex life. Discuss what you like and what you don't like. As communication improves, couples begin to recognize how many boxes they each brought into the relationship and start to dust some off, throw some away, and recycle others.

Once you feel like you can discuss your sexual script, start recreating it by engaging in physical exercises. You can start by doing Sensate Focus exercises as discussed in the chapter on *Low Libido* or read *Sex Talk* by Aline Zoldbrod and Lauren Dockett, which helps to enhance intimacy and explore new fantasies with a partner. Continue to the following activity, which outlines 30 intimate exercises to do over the course of a month. You can do them in order, or you can make a game out of it and pick a different exercise each day. Elliot and Genevieve had so much fun with these exercises, they created more of their own so they could continue to have a daily connection.

■ EXERCISE ■

Day 1 Face your partner. Take one another's hands, then jump up and down for as long as you can. Laugh, giggle, and be silly. When you stop jumping, embrace in a hug. Continuing laughing and swaying until you've gotten all of the giggles out. Stay in the hug until your breathing has slowed and the laughs have subsided. You should feel calm and re-centered as a couple.

Day 2 Lay your head in your partner's lap while they caress your temples on the sides of your head. Switch roles after several minutes.

Day 3 Sit on the floor, legs crossed, heart to heart (facing one another). Put your hand on your partner's chest while they reciprocate. Feel each other's breath and match your breathing together. For each breath you inhale, imagine you are breathing your partner in. When you exhale, imagine you are sending them love. Each breath should be a conscious effort of accepting love and sending love. Do this for several minutes.

Day 4 Each of you select your favorite song. Then dance with one another while you take turns playing the songs. It doesn't matter if it's fast or slow. Make eye contact the whole time. If you can't pick just one favorite song, agree to dance to multiple songs.

Day 5 Lay on the floor on your back, facing the ceiling. Take your partner's hand while they take yours. Wrap your fingers together. Soak up the sensations of your partner's hand, paying close attention to the temperature and the texture. As your heart rate and your breath slow, see if you can feel the blood pumping through their veins.

Day 6 Go to your linen closet and grab several sets of sheets. Work together to build a fort out of the sheets. Grab extra blankets if necessary. Once it is finished, cuddle inside the fort. Have what I call a "living room sleepover" and sleep somewhere outside of the bedroom that night.

Day 7 Find a comfortable place to sit down facing one another. You'll also need a hard surface, so a table might be a good choice. If you prefer, you can also use a book or something hard to put on the floor or bed. You'll also need a 6-sided die for this exercise. If you don't have one, use some paper and tape to make one of your own. Roll the die and do the following for each number (or come up with your own):

1 = give each other a high five

2 = Give your partner a compliment

3 = Give each other a hug

4 = Tell your partner something positive

5 = Hold your partner's elbows in your hands

6 = Tell your partner something difficult

Day 8 Pick out your partner's outfit for the day and allow them to pick out yours. If you have time, help your partner get dressed. Then switch and have them help you get dressed.

Day 9 Are you a morning person or a night owl? Depending on what works better for your schedules, decide if you would prefer to get up early and watch the sunrise in the crisp morning light or sit together in the evening and watch the sunset as the stars make their appearance. You could watch the skyline from an open window in your house, sit on a blanket at the park, or even sit on the rooftop of your apartment complex.

Day 10 Pick out a few edible treats for you and your partner to enjoy. You may choose something sweet like chocolate, something salty like nuts, or a juicy treat like fresh strawberries. Choose approximately five different treats. Now take a treat and put it to your partner's lips. Allow them to lick it, taste it, and then eat it. Take turns feeding one another. If you want to make this exercise more erotic, wear a blindfold!

Day 11 Lay in bed. Have your partner "tuck" you in. Once they have achieved this task, discuss what was most sensual. Did they take special care to be gentle with your head? To wrap up your feet? Once you've finished relaxing in this "tucked" position, climb out of bed and "tuck" your partner in. This exercise does not have to be done before bed and can be done any time of day! If you choose to do it before bed, you may need to do this exercise over two nights since you are likely to actually fall asleep if you are the one being tucked in.

Day 12 Go for a walk with your partner for 20 minutes. Hold hands throughout the walk. Do not talk during the walk. Feel free to giggle and make eye contact as a way to communicate. Soak in the sun, feel the wind, and feel your partner's energy flow from their body and into yours. Talk about this experience once you get home.

Day 13 This exercise is about team building. Literally. Building something together. Is there a bookshelf you've been meaning to put together? A Lego set that is still sitting in a box but calling your name? A home improvement project? If you can't think of a project you want to complete, then pick up some modeling clay and mold something together. You could also get a bunch of toothpicks and glue to build a structure. Make sure you work together to create something new. Compliment your partner during this process to foster appreciation. For example, "it was such a good idea to use the toothpicks with umbrellas to help build our structure because it reminds me of that time we went to the beach."

Day 14 To prep for this exercise you may want to brush your teeth or use mouthwash. Sit very closely to your partner, facing one another, and lean in until your foreheads touch. Once you feel comfortable gazing into each other's eyes, try to match your breathing. Do this for several minutes and notice how your heart rate slows. Matching your breathing and staring into each other's souls will help you feel connected.

Day 15 Sit, stand, or lay down. You may choose to be naked or partially clothed for this exercise. Your partner should then use crayons/markers/charcoal/pen to draw you on paper. When they finish drawing you, switch, and draw them. It's okay if you aren't an artist. This exercise is about noticing your partner's curves and unique characteristics. Share your drawings with one another once you have each completed your sketch.

Day 16 Fill a tub up with warm water and soak in the tub together. Make it more relaxing by adding bubbles, essential oils, or a bath bomb to embellish the experience. You could also light candles or incense to make this exercise more romantic. Pour yourselves a glass of wine or some hot tea while you soak in the tub together. If you feel comfortable, take turns sitting between each other's legs and massage and caress one another. If this exercise feels too intimate, you can modify it by sitting in the tub together fully clothed. Just make sure you don't fill the tub up with water! You can still experience being in one space together with candles and sipping wine.

Day 17 Cook a meal together! Even better, find your favorite recipe, perhaps an old family favorite, and teach your partner how to recreate it. Then have them teach you a recipe they love. Discuss what you love about the food you are creating, why the recipe is special to you, and what memories it evokes as you bond over the meal you make. Feed each other the first bite. It will help you savor the food and feel more connected.

Day 18 Pick out a movie to watch together and hold each other throughout the movie. Bonus points if you select one of your favorite movies that your partner has yet to see.

Day 19 Plant something together. If you have a garden already, spend some time working on it as a couple. Pull weeds. Plant seeds. Water vegetables. Most importantly, work together. If it's winter, or you don't have a yard, you can go to the store together and buy some small pots and seeds. Create an herb garden. As you plant the seeds, make a wish or set a goal for your relationship. If you want to, you could write it down on a small piece of paper, roll it up, and stick it in the soil. As the herbs start to grow, consider how your relationship is also continuing to grow. If the plant doesn't survive, consider the things you need to do to continue to make your relationship grow. Just as plants need to be potted, watered, and sun-bathed, relationships need the same attention: care, effort, and energy exerted into them.

Day 20 Grab a brush and detangle spray. Sit in a chair or on the couch and have your partner sit on the floor, between your legs. Spritz the detangle spray in their hair and gently brush their hair for several minutes. If your partner is bald, then use lotion and rub it into their scalp. Switch when you are done. Discuss how it felt to be groomed and to groom your partner.

Day 21 Find a tie, rope, or a bandana. Sit down next to each other, side by side, with your legs out in front of you. Tie your left leg to your partner's right leg then stand up. Time to have a three-legged race! You must work together to race across the kitchen, the backyard, or another uncluttered space. Feel free to laugh in the process. Take your time and be careful so you do not fall down together.

Day 22 Take a shower together. Wash your partner's hair with shampoo, gently massaging their scalp, and then help them rinse the soap out. Then use conditioner and do the same thing. Switch roles and have them wash and condition your hair.

Day 23 Walk or drive to a nearby park with a playground. If you have kids, you may even have a swing set in your backyard! Take turns pushing each other on the swings. Feel your partner's fingertips on your back as they push you. Notice the wind as it whips across your face. Feel your belly drop as you swing higher and higher. After you've each had a turn, you should both sit on a swing, side by side. Hold hands and sway together on the swings. Notice the push and pull of one another as you swing.

Day 24 Set aside 30 minutes and sit down together at a table. Make sure not to have any distractions (kids, cell phones, a dog that needs to go outside, etc.). Sitting across from your partner, spend a few minutes holding hands and making eye contact. When you feel calm and connected, take a pen and write one another a thank-you note. You can prepare for this ahead of time by having store-bought thank you cards, or you can just use a piece of notebook paper. Then you can get creative, decorate the front and write your own poetic words! When you finish writing your thank-you cards, read them aloud to one another. It is important to remember what you cherish about your partner, and it is a humbling reminder to hear what someone appreciates about us. Discuss how doing this exercise in silence felt for you both.

Day 25 Go on a picnic! If the weather won't allow for it, have a picnic in your living room. You can plan and pack the meal together, each packing their favorite goodies, or you could try to pack treats for one another and surprise each other at mealtime. Make sure you pack a blanket for the picnic, even if it is in your house. It is especially important to remove distractions if you do this exercise at home. No electronics should be present, unless they are being used to play music and establish the ambiance. If you do get to picnic outside, make sure you lay down after your meal to digest, hold hands, connect, and gaze up at the clouds. Breathe in the fresh air, soak in the sun, and take in the vastness of the world around you. Think about how you and your partner stay grounded and connected despite it.

Day 26 Use your pet to connect and bring you together. If you have a furry animal, or a creature you can pet and take care of, then do so. You can play catch together with your dog, clean out the gerbil cage, brush your kitten, feed treats to your rabbits, or watch the turtle swim in the tub. If you don't have a pet, go to a local animal shelter and play with a kitten or puppy there. Not only are they adorable, but animals are known to make us feel better. If you don't have a pet, don't have access to an animal shelter, or are allergic to furry friends, then just have a conversation with your partner about what pet you would like to have, if you could. What kind of animal would you choose? Pick out a name together. If all else fails, watch cat videos on the Internet. You are bound to end up laughing and bonding over the clumsiness and cuteness!

Day 27 Give your partner a light back massage for several minutes. You may do this fully or partially clothed, or naked. If you decide to do it naked, utilize massage oils or lotion. If this exercise is too intimate, rub one another's feet or hands. Switch roles.

Day 28 Remember a week ago when you had a three-legged race? Go find the tie, rope, or bandana you used. Then gather several other things around the house that can be used to tie someone up. If you are feeling up to it, you can do this exercise naked, but all that has to be bare are your arms. Have your partner close their eyes, then tie their wrists together using a silk scarf. Let them tell you how it feels against their skin. Is it smooth? Rough? Does it tickle? Itch? Remove the silk scarf and tie a shoelace around their wrists and talk about it. Make sure not to tie anything too tightly, as the goal is not to bind your partner. As you can see, you can find anything around the house to use as a tie. Get creative if you have to and grab a long sleeved shirt, a towel, or toilet paper. Notice the textures being used. You could make this a guessing game as you discuss it. Once you have tied 5 – 10 items around your partner's wrists, switch and let them do it to you. When you complete this exercise, discuss if you felt vulnerable while doing it. You can also discuss if being tied up is something you would be interested in doing in the bedroom as part of a sexual activity.

Day 29 Play a video game or board game together. If you have a gaming system, you could choose a video game where you play on the same team and work together (such as a racing game or bowling). There are many board games that remove the competitive nature as well, so you can practice working together instead of against one another. Another game you could do together is a crossword or word search puzzle.

Day 30 Pick a song, make up a dance, and perform karaoke for one another! This activity is bound to result in lots of giggles.

Day 31 After doing 30 days of exercises, you are likely to feel closer and more connected to your partner. Discuss the exercises you enjoyed. Talk about what was easy for you throughout the last 30 days. Discuss the exercises that were difficult for you to do and why. If there were any exercises you were unable to complete, discuss why.

FANTASY

Fewer people are willing to admit to having sexual fantasies than have actually had them. If you consider that the *Merriam-Webster* definition of a fantasy is considered to be "imagination unrestricted by reality" or "fiction with a large amount of imagination in it," then *everyone* has fantasies. Nearly everyone has had a sexual one as well if we consider the wide spectrum of sexuality. A fantasy may be as simple as hoping your partner holds your hand, or longing to hear "I love you" for the first time, or the millionth time. Unfortunately, many people associate the word fantasy with deviancy, but this is inaccurate and misleading.

The most common fantasy for men *and* women is that they want to feel romantic feelings in a sexual relationship (Joyal, 2014). This may seem simple enough. It's far from deviant, and it may even surprise you to learn it is considered a fantasy. Christian Joyal's study was one of the largest studies conducted to date, with over 1,500 voluntary participants. While the sample from Joyal was over 81% heterosexual, it shows that men and women's fantasies typically align. The most *un*common fantasy for both men and women was having sex with a child under the age of

12, but that isn't to say that no one has this fantasy (with 0.8% of women and 1.8% of men admitting to this sexual fantasy).

One important distinction that the Joyal study observed: women tend to be able to discern between fantasy and desire, whereas men cannot. This needs to be acknowledged when discussing fantasy because it shows women who have aggressive or unusual fantasies, such as bondage, are less likely to want to act them out in real life, whereas men are more likely to want to live out their fantasies. Another thing the Joyal study showed is that "submission and domination themes were not only common for both men and women but they were also significantly related to each other" (Joyal, p. 328). This means that people who have fantasies of being submissive also often have fantasies of being dominated. In addition, the finding that they are common fantasies may indicate men and women who have sexual fantasies about domination and submission may actually have more sexual satisfaction than those who do not have such fantasies. This may be especially true for women. Perhaps allowing oneself to have such fantasies is an indication and reflection of their own comfort with their sexuality.

I typically see clients in my practice who discuss fantasies for one of three reasons: they need to disclose the fantasy to a partner, they have no fantasies and a lack of desire and therefore a need to create them, or they feel guilty and ashamed for being aroused by the fantasy they have created. Regardless of why it's being discussed, typically the first step is to take the box off the shelf and to normalize it. Of the countless people who fantasize, many believe their fantasies are abnormal or weird. It usually surprises them to hear they are not the only one with their fantasy.

Case study: Tara and Jeff

Tara, a young woman in her mid-20s, was an editor for a local newspaper. She looked like a model with her long blond hair, slim figure, and chic wardrobe. She came in distressed after six months of marriage. Tara's primary complaint was low libido. Part of working through her low libido was exploring her history of fantasy and self-pleasure. Tara shyly admitted she had never masturbated or had a fantasy.

Trying to normalize things, I asked Tara if she ever had any career aspirations. She answered easily as she shared that she had always dreamed of being a writer. Her passion for writing eventually led her to discover her passion for editing. Using this level of comfort that had been established, I pushed Tara further and asked what her hopes and dreams were for her and her husband Jeff. "Well," she pondered, and then gushed as she talked about their future together, "we definitely want kids. But first we want to travel more. We love traveling. It's how we met and why we fell in love."

Using the information Tara had provided, we capitalized on this to help her create a fantasy. I asked her to describe what her dream vacation looked like. I watched Tara's face light up as she described her perfect vacation, where she and Jeff travel to Belize together and lay on the beach ordering cocktails with little umbrellas in them. Throughout the discussion, I pushed Tara to add details to the fantasy. What was she wearing? What was Jeff wearing? How did the air smell? How did the sand feel on the beach? Was it loose and smooth? Or was it wet and stuck together? As Tara closed her eyes and pieced together the details, her face changed. She took a deep breath in, as if to smell the ocean breeze, then opened her eyes and gushed, "I think I can do this!" It suddenly clicked to her that she was able to fantasize, and in fact had fantasized, but had not categorized it as such.

As Tara incorporated all the details into the fantasy, she realized that she just needed to add a sexual component in order to create a *sexual* fantasy. This realization actually excited her and over the next few weeks she embraced this aspect of herself, creating a whole box of fantasies. As she shared her fantasy with her husband, it created a new dialogue between them. The dialogue and open communication created sexual desire between them. Tara felt empowered knowing she was in control of creating her own fantasies, and was excited at the sexual energy that sparked between her and Jeff.

For those that do not currently have fantasies, I encourage you to create one. Again, a fantasy can be as simple as thinking about you and your partner being on vacation at a ski resort. Once some form of fantasy becomes comfortable, elaborate on it. For many people, fantasy can open their world to more enhancing self-pleasure and partner relations. The exercise at the end of this chapter will help you.

It is also important to have a discussion with your partner about the decision whether to share fantasies. Many people have fantasies they would never want to actually live out. An example of an extreme fantasy is women who imagine being raped. In reality, they would never wish for this to happen (and if it does they may blame their fantasy for it occurring in real life. Rape is *never* the victim's fault—please read more in the *Sexual Assault, Abuse, and Trauma* chapter). This is a fantasy a person might choose to keep private because they may feel embarrassed or ashamed to admit to this kind of fantasy. This is exactly why fantasies need to be normalized, because people feel ashamed or embarrassed to have fantasies in the first place.

Case study: Brad

Brad found his way into my office after he took his sexual fantasy too far. When Brad had his first therapy appointment he was feeling ashamed, embarrassed, and overwhelmed. He was not sure where to start during his first session, so I encouraged him to start at the beginning. He stumbled his way through his story, starting with his childhood, and shared a recollection of sniffing his mother's panties when he was seven years old. Brad didn't remember why he sniffed them, but he does remember he got caught, and never did it again. The embarrassment he felt at such a young age swept over him in my office, an experience of enjoying humiliation. After this experience, Brad shared that he tried to hide any sexual urges that seemed "out of the norm" for decades. He chose not to be vulnerable and shut this box.

While pursuing a career in law enforcement, Brad met his wife, a retail manager, on a blind date when they were both in their early 20s. They connected instantaneously, bonding over common interests such as their love for wine, live music, and biking. Brad was attracted to Kate's petite figure and girl-next-door innocence, while Kate was attracted to his dominance and sense of humor. When he married his Kate, he engaged in and maintained a scripted sex life for many years. Typically he would initiate, having the higher sex drive, and they'd engage in intercourse negligent of foreplay.

Despite viewing one another as equals, they maintained fairly traditional gender roles, although both worked hard for their careers. After having two children, their sex life waned. The couple had to get creative, carving time out of their busy schedules to find a way to be intimate. They both felt it was an important part of the marriage and would stay up late to have sex after the kids went to bed.

After their kids moved out of the house, they realized their sex life had taken a nosedive as far as frequency, but they finally felt free to reconnect. They no longer had to tiptoe around late at night, suffocating the sounds of an orgasm into a pillow. They introduced sex toys and props into their sex life, and Brad felt his old fantasies begin to resurface. He had tried to suppress his fantasies for many years, saving them for when he masturbated. When he and Kate started having a more active sex life again, and were taking more sexual risks, it was almost as if the floodgates had opened. Brad tried to initiate role-play into their sex life, and Kate begrudgingly tried it a few times. She came home from work one day and Brad had managed to tie himself up to their bed, wearing nothing but high heels and a lacy red thong. He felt the same humiliation and excitement he had experienced when he was found sniffing his mother's underpants. Kate was very uncomfortable, feeling as if Brad no longer needed her as part of his sexual repertoire. He was creating a fantasy world without her input.

Unfortunately, Kate felt so uncomfortable that she closed the door on any kind of kink. There were no more vibrators, no more props, and role-play was out of the question. Brad began to search for other ways to fulfill his sexual needs and took to online forums. He posted ads from time to time, seeking someone who would dominate and humiliate him. Brad didn't share this with Kate—he didn't plan to actually engage with someone in real life. But the responses he received were just as thrilling and exciting for him.

It was all fun and games until someone responded to Brad's ad, requesting money and threatening to contact Brad's wife and kids and tell them about his "perverse" ways. Humiliated beyond the fantasy, Brad told Kate what happened. The same night they sent the mysterious person money, they also scheduled a therapy appointment.

Things had gotten out of hand, and both Brad and Kate had contributed to the dilemma due to his secrecy and her lack of acceptance. Perhaps if Brad had been able to share his own fanta-sies in a more transparent and non-demanding way, Kate might have been more open to experiencing them together. While Kate felt too many boundaries had been crossed by the time the couple sought therapy, she was able to bring herself to listen to Brad and try to understand his sexual desires. She was firm that she did not want to live them out, but was also firm that she would accept him without judgment. Brad's fantasy would stay just that, yet he and Kate felt closer than they had in years. Much of the closeness they felt was related to the couple's ability to be vulnerable with one another.

I often encourage people to share fantasies with their part-ners to enliven their sexual script and create desire between them. Even if the couple never acts out the fantasy, it shows a person's creative and playful side, and may contribute to their flirtatious and sexual side. A conversation about fantasies is based on trust and needs to be free of judgment. This can be a vulner-able conversation and you need to trust that your partner will listen without shame.

When people are concerned about their partner judging and shaming them, but need to share their sexual fantasy because they have kept it to themselves their entire lives, they may seek a sex therapist to help navigate the conversation. People are often surprised, and feel relieved, after they discuss their fantasies with a partner and are accepted without judgment. This is true even if their partner never engages in the fantasy.

The next question: how do you share a sexual fantasy with a partner? When people have something important to discuss with their partner, especially something sexually related, it is impera-tive to discuss it in a neutral setting when you both are calm and getting along. Sharing a deep fantasy while naked in bed makes both of you even more vulnerable and can create an awkward and needlessly uncomfortable moment. Your partner may think you want them to exhibit the behavior and act out the fantasy in that moment. This is too much pressure for the first time it is discussed. Additionally, if they say no and you become offended, then both people end up being hurt.

That being said, if you have engaged in some discussion with your partner before, and they feel comfortable saying no to you if they feel uncomfortable and it will not ruin your mood or the moment, go ahead and ask them to (insert desired behavior here). Otherwise, I encourage you to utilize the exercises at the end of this chapter.

■ EXERCISE ■

The Pancake Talk is a unique technique I created as a useful way to have difficult conversations with anyone. It's easy: you just discuss something difficult, like your sexual fantasy, over pancakes! While this may sound silly, the point is that there is nothing controversial about delicious, syrupy pancakes (unless your partner is gluten intolerant). Additionally, most people eat pancakes at the kitchen table, a neutral setting. In contrast, the bedroom is typically a place of intimacy. Fortunately, pancakes are anything but.

Vulnerable discussions about sex should never take place where the couple is intimate, nor just after intimacy occurs. The Pancake Talk encourages couples to have difficult conversations the following morning, not while they are vulnerable and naked in bed just after having sex. Given time to reflect and to have a conversation in the kitchen the following day, over pancakes, creates an atmosphere more conducive to having a productive conversation about a difficult topic. The Pancake Talk: helping people to stop waffling one flip at a time.

■ EXERCISE ■

In this exercise, you will create a sexual fantasy. If you have never had a sexual fantasy before or are unsure how to indulge in the world of fantasy, this exercise is for you! First, you will need a pen and paper to complete this exercise. Make sure you find a comfortable surface to write on and a place to sit. Take 20 minutes to free-write and describe a fantasy. You can write whatever comes to mind. It doesn't have to be a fantasy *you* have, but it should be sexual in nature. If you can't think of a fantasy of your own, pretend you are writing an erotic story for a website. It's okay if this writing exercise feels silly or juvenile. The goal is to tap into a creative part of your brain that you have not used before.

Alternatively, you can do this exercise as a couple's talking exercise. If you select this option, you should be comfortable talking together about things sexual in nature. Create a sensual space to talk, such as the bathtub or by the fireplace. You might have this discussion over a glass of wine or near the fireplace. When you are ready, one of you should start by creating a "scene." After a sentence or two, the other person should continue the story with a sentence or two. Continue to switch back and forth as the scene gets spicier and sexier. Just as with the writing exercise, this conversational storytelling doesn't have to be a fantasy of your own. It is about creating an erotic story together, having fun, and connecting in a new and erotic way. This exercise may even lead you right to the bedroom!

SEXUAL ASSAULT, ABUSE, AND TRAUMA

One in four girls will be sexually assaulted by the time they are 18 years old. According to the non-profit organization RAINN (Rape, Abuse, and Incest National Network), one in six women will be a victim of rape, or attempted rape, in their lifetime, compared to one in 33 men. While these numbers are staggering, they may be even higher as many people who are sexually assaulted never make a report or tell anyone. This is particularly true for boys and men who are told to like sex and to want it at the drop of a hat.

As a therapist, I encounter people who have suffered from sexual assault and rape, and who long to have a healthy sexual relationship with an intimate partner. I want to help women have a voice and own their sexuality. Yet so many women I meet who have been sexually assaulted and are unable to feel like sexual beings. They feel like victims. They feel like their sexuality has been taken from them, put in a box and sealed away, and they are unsure how to open that box.

Domestic violence, which includes physical, sexual, emotional, verbal, and psychological abuse, is another type of trauma people may experience. The National Coalition Against Domestic Violence, a non-profit organization focused on public policy change, further defines domestic violence as the "willful intimidation, physical assault, battery, sexual assault, and/or other abusive behavior as part of a systematic pattern of power and control perpetrated by one intimate partner against another" (2018). In the United States it is estimated that ten million people a year are victims of physical violence from an intimate partner, equating to 20 people per minute. Furthermore, more than 20,000 phone calls are made daily to domestic violence hotlines, as victims seek advice and help to leave an abusive situation.

Leaving an abusive relationship can be more difficult than staying in one. The victim may experience additional threats and forms of violence, forcing them to stay in their current situation. If a victim is dependent on the abuser financially, and they have been isolated from family and friends, they may stay rather than be homeless. Abusers may threaten to get full custody of kids when children are involved. Leaving an abusive relationship could be a life-or-death situation for many.

When a victim finds the strength and ability to leave an abusive relationship, they may discover local shelters have a limited number of beds. Domestic violence shelters are nearly always full, and frequently people are turned away for services. Male and trans victims often do not have the option to stay at shelters. There are not enough resources to meet the needs of the many abused and assaulted in many communities. Sadly, many towns do not even have a safe place for men and women fleeing domestic violence or sexual assault to go. It is even more difficult for those who identify as lesbian, gay, or transgender to seek services, as they may be discriminated against and turned away.

Sexual assault and domestic violence occurs frequently in our society, but they are also personal, private, and difficult topics for people to address. Many victims have feelings of shame and guilt for not being able to leave a situation sooner, and internalize the violent messages they were told by the abuser. However, it is important to discuss so it does not stall someone's sexuality and well-being. Harboring a secret may cause more damage over time to someone's sense of sexuality. Addressing it may help a person heal and feel empowered. That being said, the journey of sexual assault and abuse is personal for everyone and there is no right or wrong way to address it.

For some people it is an issue they deal with daily and it affects all aspects of their lives. It may be difficult to leave the house because there are so many triggers they experience. They may push their sexuality aside to avoid being triggered by past trauma. For others, sexual assault and abuse does not become an issue until they are in a loving and committed relationship. Having a person in your life who supports you and treats you well can be confusing if you've been given messages that you're worthless and your body is a sexual object.

For those who can relate to the former, I will assume you have picked this book up because you are ready to own your sexuality. You may realize that something was stolen from you, or feel that you are missing out on something. The good news is that while you may not be in touch with your sexuality, no one can take it from you. Your sexuality is part of *who* you are, even when you suppress it, and it's still on the shelf waiting for you to open the box. Perhaps it says even more about your sexuality when you do suppress it. Just because we do not discuss something does not erase it or make it non-existent. Your sexuality is *yours* and *yours only*. Perhaps your sexuality went into hiding as a way to protect you. Honor your sexuality, and yourself, as it begins to resurface.

How do you even begin to reinstate your sexuality to achieve liberation? First, it begins with discussing the sexual assault and abuse. This can be difficult if it is a secret that has never been told to anyone, worse if you told someone but they didn't believe you. This part of the journey is about healing. There is not a right or wrong way to start this process but it has to start with you. Sex therapist Wendy Maltz encourages people to constantly remind themselves that "you are pursing sexual healing *for yourself*—you are reaching *your* goals, at *your* pace, for *your* benefit. The motivation to heal needs to come from within yourself" (Maltz, 2012, p. 78).

The first time you decide to talk about your assault, you should do it in a safe space with someone you trust. This may be with a therapist, a partner, a friend, or in a support group. Perhaps it begins with you just saying out loud what happened, acknowledging the assault occurred. Trust yourself and your memories.

Saying you were assaulted out loud for the first time can be vulnerable and scary. You may feel guilt, shame, embarrassment, sadness, or anger. It is important that you are in a safe space because you may be entering unknown territory. Everyone reacts differently ,and talking about your assault may cause you to have flashbacks, anxiety, or fear.

Flashbacks refer to having images of the assault in your head. The flashback may be very brief, or it may linger like a bad dream. There may be a trigger that prompts the flashback, such as seeing someone who looks like the person who assaulted you, or smelling the same cologne the offender wore. For many, there is no identifying trigger. Flashbacks can come seemingly out of nowhere. They may cause you to feel anxious or scared. Please note that this is perfectly normal. If reading this is causing some anxiety, it is okay to put the book down and take a break. If you want to keep reading, stop for a moment to take a deep breath. Breathe. Inhale deeply, exhale *slowly*. Breathe in. Breathe out.

Anxiety can be a scary and nerve-wracking feeling. It can feel overwhelming. For some, feelings of anxiety can become so intense that they induce a panic attack. Panic attacks stem from anxiety, but they can be debilitating. Oftentimes they are associated with symptoms similar to a heart attack: tight chest, heavy breathing, and cold sweats.

If you think you are having a panic attack, or you are prone to having them, the most important thing you can do is remember to *breathe*. This is almost always easier said than done, but it is the most important thing you can do for yourself. If you have a friend or partner available, they can help to relieve the anxiety and calm you down by talking in a soft voice, encouraging you to continue breathing, rubbing your back (if you feel safe being touched), encouraging you to make eye contact, and having you take small sips of water. If you frequently experience debilitating panic attacks, it is recommended that you speak to a therapist. You may also need to be referred to a psychiatrist who can prescribe anxiety-reducing medication.

Another emotion one might experience when acknowledging their sexual assault is fear. If fear of being hurt again by someone is a reality, consider what is best for your safety before proceeding. Some people are not able to discuss abuse or reach out for help while they are still with their abuser because it actually makes the situation more unsafe. *Always* put your safety (and your children's, if they are a factor) first.

Case study: Sarah and Judd

For those of you who are in a healthy relationship and are now being triggered by past events, this can be a difficult journey. I have seen many clients who became very confused when past trauma threatened their healthy relationship. As one client, Sarah, stated, "I thought I had dealt with this. I thought I was over it, or at least had forgotten about it."

Sometimes being in a healthy relationship allows a person to finally feel safe enough to confront their history of trauma and abuse. However, they must have the support of their partner as they go through this process. Sarah felt awful that she was making her partner Judd go through this experience with her. "This is my past—he shouldn't have to deal with it. I don't want to have sex anymore because I keep having flashbacks. I am worried he is going to leave me because we haven't had sex in almost three months," she shared during her first therapy session.

Sarah and Judd had been together for two years. They worked at the same tech company and met through a chance encounter in the break room. The first year and a half of the relationship they had great sex. "But it was like everything changed once Judd moved in," Sarah confided. Suddenly, sex was uncomfortable, even painful at times, for Sarah. She couldn't figure out what had changed, until one night they were attempting intercourse and all of a sudden Sarah experienced a flashback. She made an appointment the next day after she had recalled vivid details of being abused by a babysitter when she was six years old.

"It's all I've been thinking about the last week," Sarah shared, elaborating that these memories were resurfacing and she was not sure what to do with the internal chaos. "I don't know why this is all coming up—I blocked it out for decades. I mean, I knew it happened, but I haven't thought about it in years, especially in such detail. Suddenly, I feel like I'm reliving it and there are moments with Judd when I feel six years old again." Sarah had experienced a phenomenon called *dissociation*, where a memory is not forgotten but is in a storage box and is later recalled.

As Sarah elaborated about her upbringing, she discussed the details she was able to recall about the assault. She had never told anyone because her mother had been emotionally abusive and her father was in and out of her life. The babysitter had also threatened her if she told anyone, so she never did—until now.

The reason the assault was resurfacing so intensely was because of Sarah's solid relationship with Judd. It may sound like an oxymoron: why would Sarah's healthy relationship trigger memories of the assault? For Sarah, it was the first time she felt safe enough to remember the details of the assault. As a small girl, she did not feel safe, heard, loved, or protected ,so she kept the assault a secret.

Finally feeling safe enough to address the assault allowed Sarah to begin to heal. With therapeutic interventions, she was able to separate the assault triggers from intimacy with Judd. She was also able to utilize Judd's positive support and demeanor to help her heal.

Perhaps you do not have a support system and are not ready to voice aloud, or in detail, what happened to you yet. Another way to start the healing process is through journaling or drawing. There is scientific evidence that shows journaling can reduce stress, effectively solve problems, and clarify thoughts and feelings you may be experiencing. This form of expression can also help desensitize the traumatic experience, making it easier to talk about.

James Pennebaker created the Expressive Writing Paradigm in the 1980s, after doing research on the healthy affects of journaling about traumatic events. Pennebaker's instructions are simple: write about a traumatic event for 15 minutes per day for three days. Specifically, Pennebaker and Chung (2011, p.419) instruct participants to do the following:

> For the next 3 days, I would like for you to write about your very deepest thoughts and feelings about the most traumatic experience of your entire life. In your writing, I'd like you to really let go and explore your very deepest emotions and thoughts. You might tie this trauma to your childhood, your relationships with others, including parents, lovers, friends or relatives. You may also link this event to your past, your present

*or your future, or to who you have been, who you
would like to be, or who you are now. You may write
about the same general issues or experiences on all
days of writing or about different topics each day.
Not everyone has had a single trauma but all of us
have had major conflicts or stressors—and you can
write about these as well. All of your writing will be
completely confidential. Don't worry about spelling,
sentence structure, or grammar. The only rule is that
once you begin writing, continue to do so until your
time is up.*

While Pennebaker states that people can reap benefits after
only three days of doing this activity, I would encourage you to
continue journaling daily if it feels beneficial. Some people will
not be able to start writing about their trauma right away. That's
okay. Write about your week, or why you chose to decorate your
room the way you did, or your favorite kind of pizza. If that's a
safer place to start, then start there. Just get comfortable writing.
Once you feel comfortable writing, and feel safe doing so, then
you can start to write about your past. While writing alone is not
likely to resolve a person's complex history, it is a starting point to
acknowledge that you in fact have a complex history. It puts the
trauma on paper. You can allow the paper to take on your burden
so you do not have to continue to carry it around by yourself.

However you decide to move forward, addressing trauma and
assault is okay. Writing is just one option. Therapy is another
one. The following exercises are additional options and may help
guide you to find healing.

▪ EXERCISE ▪

You are probably familiar with the scene from the popular '90s movie *Good Will Hunting* when Robin Williams's character places his hands on the protagonist, played by Matt Damon, and begins to say, "It's not your fault." Initially defensive, the protagonist quickly breaks down into tears. He finally feels validated, heard, and trusts someone enough to be able to be vulnerable. Well, Robin Williams is right, IT'S NOT YOUR FAULT. This exercise is about forgiving yourself for any blame you take for the assault or trauma you experienced.

Find a safe place, get comfortable, take a deep breath, and write a letter to the you who was assaulted. Reach out to them. Tell them how you feel. Ask those questions filled with self-blame. Offer forgiveness. Show compassion. Write, write, and write some more. You deserve to reach out to yourself and tell yourself how you feel.

▪ EXERCISE ▪

Drawing pictures of your experiences can be another outlet to work through trauma. It is a form of "self-expression that made revealing painful thoughts and feelings much less threatening" (Oster, 2004, p. xvi). The pictures you draw do not have to be of people or places, although they may be. They can be abstract and representative of your past, present, or future, as you create "internal perceptions about self and the world" (Malchiodi, 2011, p.179). The idea of "art expression provides a nonverbal, sensory-based approach to contain and alleviate feelings of internal distress, chaos, and helplessness that a woman may be urgently experiencing related to her abuse" (Malchiodi, 2011, p. 342).

Drawing, as a way of processing, also serves to create a safe space to be able to review and interpret your own artwork versus having someone analyze it for you. You can then express "emotions and ideas that otherwise they could not easily describe" (Oster, 2004, p. 3). Trying to put trauma into words may be too difficult in therapy and discussing a drawing may be both easier and safer. "Drawings contribute greatly to this therapeutic process where safe outlets of one's self in a free space without fears or constraints is a primary key toward health" (Oster, 2004, p. 151).

So, grab yourself a sketchpad and try Oster and Malchiodi's therapeutic drawing techniques. Be sure to reflect on your drawings once you are done with them. Show them to someone else if you feel comfortable. What does your drawing mean? Is your drawing abstract? Concrete? What colors did you choose to convey the message? Feel free to draw as many pictures as you want, to capture the range of emotions you are feeling as you process your own trauma.

NONSEXUAL RELATIONSHIPS

It is estimated that about one in five marriages are nonsexual (McCarthy, 2014). A relationship is considered nonsexual when couples are intimate less than ten times per year. For some couples, this works. Being sexual may not be a stabilizer for their relationship. This is not to say that these couples are not connected physically or aren't intimate. They are just not sexual. Couples in nonsexual relationships who have negotiated intimacy in other ways don't tend to seek out sex therapy.

Couples who do come to see me for issues related to a nonsexual marriage often feel stuck. They have not been sexual in a long time and they do not know how to open this box, or where to start to reawaken this part of their relationship. Sometimes, the issue is related to low libido. Oftentimes, it's related to other issues within the relationship.

Case study: Stella and Nate

Stella and Nate had been together for 25 years, and married for 22. Together they had four children, and their youngest had moved out of the house a year ago. They lived in a large house in the suburbs, and vacationed at their summer home in Colorado.

Nate was a successful heart surgeon, while Stella had stayed home to raise their children. Until recently, they displayed very traditional gender roles. After 25 years, there was very little keeping them together and they had nothing in common aside from the fact that they lived together.

It was Nate's idea to seek out therapy. The couple was only intimate about twice a year, a pattern for at least the last five years. The issue had become more blaring after their children moved out, which exacerbated the fact that they had so little in common.

During an individual session with Nate to learn more about his perspective of the marriage, he said, "I don't actually think I need therapy. I just need you to fix my wife." This is a phrase I have heard frequently. When this occurs, I have to explain to clients that *all* issues are couple's issues. While the problem may be more engrained in one person, it surely will not be fixed without both partners putting in effort, to support their partner if nothing else.

Nate was hesitant to believe he could assist in any way, but he wanted his sex life back. "When we started dating, Stella was a sex machine. Sometimes I think she just put forward this farce so I'd marry her and she could have my money." This was a harsh statement, but also something to explore with Stella.

When confronted in her own individual session, Stella actually agreed. "I don't think it was intentional, but I was young and ready to be a mother. I knew Nate would be a good provider. After we had kids, sex just wasn't a priority anymore." Being menopausal, Stella admitted to having low libido, but with further exploration it was evident it was more than just that. "I started avoiding sex years ago. I would wake up and Nate would be having sex with me. I haven't had an orgasm in years. I don't even know what being wet feels like anymore. I want to stay with Nate. It's not even an option to leave. I'll do what I have to do to make this work."

This was the first time Stella had shared that Nate had assaulted her, although it was difficult for her to see it that way because it was her husband. It took many sessions for Stella to process this, but she knew she had to work through this if she wanted to desire Nate again in a sexual manner.

It was time to confront Nate. He recalled he had been intimate with Stella while she was sleeping. "She said sex was too much work, so I was trying to make things easier for her," he said ignorantly but also genuinely. Nate was never trying to assault his wife. His lack of awareness had caused harm to Stella and it was imperative for him to accept his actions and how they affected her. It took many sessions for Nate to grieve and work through his own remorse.

While Nate and Stella each did individual work to address their trauma and acknowledge the reasons which had brought them to a sexless marriage, they continued to be nonsexual. This was in fact a request by me, but one that they readily agreed to. They needed to heal individually and as a couple before they could connect again physically. When the couple was ready to try being intimate again, they took baby steps to reach success.

Couples experiencing nonsexual marriages cannot be expected to just start having sex again after not being intimate for many months or years. The first step is to establish their goal as a couple. For Nate, it was to be intimate with his wife at least twice a month. For Stella it was to find sex tolerable and reconnect with her husband. The next step to reconnection, aside from the individual work they both did, was communication and rebuilding trust. Their focus for so many years had been on their children. Now that they couldn't distract themselves with that anymore, they had to find new material. They decided to start by picking a new activity to try together. Initially scared of reconnecting, they avoided this homework assignment for a few weeks but I encouraged them to prioritize the activity, and ultimately their relationship. The activity wasn't really about trying something new so much as what it symbolized: a new beginning and connection.

When they were ready, Stella and Nate attended a play at a local theater. This allowed them the opportunity to be in an environment where they did not have to create an experience because the experience was created for them. Ultimately, seeing a play together fostered discussion as they critiqued what they enjoyed about the show, and what they did not like. It was a start. Eventually, with continued therapy and communication, the couple created new boxes and moved on to more intimate exercises like Sensate Focus, outlined at the end of the *Low Libido* chapter. Stella took the time to get to know her body, which helped her relax and feel safe being intimate with Nate. Nate respected Stella's boundaries, which further created trust and intimacy.

Rekindling desire is as simple, or complicated, as the reasons that led to the lack of desire in the first place. Oftentimes, couples are forced to examine other issues within their relationship which led to the lack of desire and the nonsexual relationship. It is important to emphasize, as with many issues, that this is a couples issue. Blaming one person, as Nate initially tried to do with Stella, is not only ineffective but can cause further tension and distrust.

Case study: Caitlin and Alyssa

Caitlin and Alyssa, a lesbian couple in their early forties, came to see me for assistance in creating desire in their relationship. Caitlin was a software analyst and Alyssa was a social worker working part time. They had a daughter together and described their relationship as healthy, except their sex life. We spent their first two sessions discussing their relationship: how they met, how they fought, and how they parented. They genuinely did have a healthy relationship consisting of quality time together and good communication. Sometimes people come to therapy just to seek some general direction and advice when they feel stuck. "Stuck is exactly how we feel," Caitlin shared, holding Alyssa's hand as she nodded in agreement.

"It's like we have just gotten so bogged down with responsibilities that we forget to prioritize each other, and as a result our sex life has suffered," Alyssa confirmed. They shared life goals and had a solid foundation in their relationship. They had just forgotten how to be playful.

Therefore, their first assignment was a playful one. "I want you to make out," I directed them. Caitlin looked at me questioningly and smirked. She laughed and said "Then what?"

"That's all," I offered, then I elaborated, "To rekindle desire, we first need to create desire." They were to give one another an elongated kiss, in the morning, or before bed. The important piece of this assignment was that it was not to lead to anything more sexual. The kiss itself was to create a lingering feeling of wanting and desiring to do it more. "Do you share a kiss before you leave for the day?" I asked.

"Of course we do," shot Caitlin.

"But it's just a peck on the lips," admitted Alyssa. This is what I had anticipated their answer would be. I encouraged them to share an elongated kiss on their way out the door in the morning. There's nothing sexy about a peck on the lips after you've been together for years. For many couples it's almost second nature, habit, and while it's cute, it's not sexy. There are typically few feelings associated with it and it becomes as mundane as patting a child on the head. Certainly those feelings will not lead to intimacy in the bedroom.

McCarthy confirms that touching must occur both in the bedroom and outside of it. In his workshops, he explains that "contrary to the myth that 'horniness' occurs after not being sexual for weeks, desire is facilitated by a regular rhythm of sexual activity. When sex is less than twice a month, you can become self-conscious and fall into a cycle of anticipatory anxiety, tense and unsatisfying sex, and avoidance." This is the pattern Caitlin and Alyssa had fallen into.

As elaborated upon in the *Low Libido* chapter, I also encouraged this couple to try David Schnarch's hugging till relaxed exercise, which turns a simple hug into a vulnerable and intimate act. Since Caitlin was considered the "initiator" when the couple was intimate, this exercise was Alyssa's assignment to initiate.

Another key component to creating desire is to encourage the person with low-libido to start initiating. Why would someone with low-libido, avoiding intimacy, initiate if they have no interest in being intimate? They wouldn't, because their needs are being met. The goal of the hugging exercise is to create desire and stir the libido in the person with no desire, and this evolves into being motivated to want to initiate intimacy. It's much less intimidating to initiate a hug with your partner, than to feel pressured to jump into bed with them. If this also feels like pressure, I ask couples to schedule a time to do the exercise so neither of them feels pressure to initiate.

For this exercise, Alyssa had to initiate by giving Caitlin a hug. I usually tell couples to take this exercise at face value when I first assign it. I acknowledge that it sounds silly and simplistic. I want them to be able to laugh over this exercise, and laugh at me for giving it to them. One thing about assigning homework to couples is that, even if the couple thinks the exercise is "silly" or "stupid," neither has to take responsibility for it. "Well, our therapist said we had to, so we might as well give it a shot." Secretly, couples like being given some direction when they feel lost in their relationship.

I encourage couples to do this exercise at face value until the person who was assigned to be the initiator feels comfortable. Interestingly, although this exercise is very simplistic and straightforward, I am often surprised when couples avoid doing it. Some say it's just "stupid" and they "don't see the point." They will ask, "Why did you even assign us this exercise?" To me, the bigger question is, why didn't you do the exercise? I will calmly explain that I was trying to offer them a superficial exercise that was not intimidating and would allow them time to reconnect. Again, you can't go from zero to 60, and a hugging exercise for a couple that has not been intimate and has a lack of desire should take baby steps. However, as Schnarch points out, "Hugging till relaxed isn't easy to do with real depth," (2009, p. 160), meaning it can be done "superficially."

In short, what Schnarch is encouraging couples to do is let themselves go in their partner's arms, while also being attentive to one's own needs and recognizing their own feelings and emotions during the process. It can be a very intense exercise to let yourself go. The purpose, I explain to my questioning clients, is to trust, be open, and let yourself go, all while maintaining yourself. Suddenly, a simplistic hug isn't so simple.

Once couples feel secure in doing Schnarch's hugging till relaxed exercise, I will introduce them to Sensate Focus exercises, which were also reviewed in the *Low Libido* chapter. Meanwhile, couples will also be working on communication exercises to help them reconnect. Please read the *Communication* chapter for more elaborate exercises on communication.

It should be noted that recreating desire in a relationship is work. It is hard work that takes a valiant effort. A couple must be committed to making change and bettering their relationship. They must be willing to throw away boxes, recycle others, and fill new ones together. The effort to fill new boxes together must be conscious and genuine. It can be scary and intimidating to reconnect with a person and feel vulnerable, but the rewards for allowing another into your heart are vast. In addition, we all deserve to feel desire and pleasure. You owe it to yourself to reconnect with your partner.

■ EXERCISE ■

When things become mundane and habitual in a relationship, we might not remember what desire looks or feels like. Get a pen and paper and think back to the beginning of your relationship. Recall what it felt like to truly feel desired, and how it felt to express your own desires. Journal these thoughts. You may even start to feel yourself throbbing or pulsing at the thought.

Did you stop acting on those impulses over time? Well, it's time to reconnect with them. To start creating desire, ask yourself: what makes you feel desired? Write down your ideas. Some people feel desired when someone tells them how sexy they look. Other people feel desired when their partner comes up behind them and takes them into a warm embrace.

Have you ever expressed to your partner what makes you feel extra special and desired? Do you know what makes your partner feel desired? Have you asked them? Do you make an effort to show them you desire them? After you reflect and journal your ideas, consider sharing these intimate thoughts with your partner, utilizing the Pancake Talk from the *Fantasy* chapter.

EARLY EJACULATION

Early ejaculation, sometimes called premature ejaculation, is an unwanted response that occurs in sexual situations. Most people refer to it as "cumming too quickly." To be considered a medical condition a man must ejaculate in under two minutes. For it to be considered a sexuality issue, it must be causing some sort of distress. Since the average length of penile-vaginal intercourse is only seven minutes, it is often expected that a man will experience some form of early ejaculation at some point in time. Often, this occurs due to over-excitement and some sort of anxiety related to the relationship: stress, or low self-esteem. It is estimated that only 2–5% of men actually meet the clinical diagnosis for early ejaculation.

Men that seek my services for early ejaculation often are not considered to have an issue that meets the clinical diagnosis, but it is estimated that between 20–60% of men feel it is an issue that is impacting their sex lives. The complaint is often more generic, with a desire to want to "last longer" and a feeling that they ejaculate too quickly. Even more often, it is not an issue their partner has complained about but something the man feels self-conscious about. In 2009, Cory Silverberg wrote a blog stating:

> *The idea of premature ejaculation presupposes that
> there is a clear end goal, and that you're getting there
> too soon. It also presupposes that extending sex is an
> obvious goal of sex. If you're ejaculating before you
> want to, or before your partner wants to, the first thing
> you ought to do is ask yourself, what is it that I want
> to extend? Is the sex I'm having good enough to want
> to make it last longer? Am I coming quickly because
> really, there's not much to wait around for? And do
> I want the goal I set for sex to be one that requires a
> stopwatch to evaluate? What if all you wanted from a
> sexual encounter was to feel good?*

Case study: Travis

When Travis, a 25-year-old heterosexual man, sought me out for therapy, he said he was ejaculating within the two-minute time frame. He worked doing road construction which was labor-intensive, but allowed him to make good money and didn't require him to travel for work. Travis said he had been in a serious relationship for two years, but the relationship ended due to his infidelity. He had been dating casually for the last year since the break-up. Travis said things never went beyond a one-night stand with women he met because he would ejaculate "too quickly." According to him, he did meet the clinical diagnosis for early ejaculation. Feelings of embarrassment made Travis feel like a failure. He had begun to avoid dating completely.

About three months prior to seeing me, Travis met Kristina, a 26-year-old teacher, through a mutual friend. Travis said they got along well, had fun together, and shared common interests. He confided he thought Kristina might be "the one." When I asked about their sex life, Travis reported he and Kristina started having sex after about three weeks.

Although they were currently sexually active, he was worried Kristina was going to break up with him because of his ejaculation issues. She had never said this to him. In fact, he said Kristina had been really positive and encouraging about their sex life and had never complained about it. Travis felt like the early ejaculation was his issue and he admitted to using a topical gel and a pill he bought at an adult store, to try to resolve it. After little success with the gel or the pill, he shared that he had begun to avoid sex with Kristina because it was giving him so much anxiety.

Kristina had noticed his avoidance and he was running out of excuses not to spend time with her. In fact, he wanted nothing more than to spend time with Kristina, but he didn't feel worthy of her time. Travis had begun to feel so inadequate that he sought therapy, but didn't tell Kristina he was doing so. He didn't want to feel any more weak and vulnerable than he already did.

Travis was unwilling to open up to Kristina about his insecurities, but he was able to open up in therapy. He felt like Kristina was "too good" for him because she had a college degree and he did not. He also admitted he still felt a lot of guilt from cheating in his prior relationship and thought the premature ejaculation was how he was being punished. To him, it was a clear sign he didn't deserve someone like Kristina.

There were additional pressures he felt at his job and the expectations from his supervisor were weighing on him. He admitted he was physically exhausted from doing physical labor every day. Travis said that work gave him anxiety and he had a fear of being dispensable. To stay more alert at work he had turned to energy drinks and admitted to smoking cigarettes with co-workers during his lunch breaks.

When the conversation turned to sex, it turned out Travis was having such anxiety about maintaining an erection that he was actually losing his erection. He was desperate for resolution and open to change. For many men, early ejaculation can actually turn into erectile dysfunction. The anxiety and pressure to perform becomes so overwhelming that the penis suddenly is unable to perform at all.

Before we dove into things, I encouraged Travis to consider who was judging him. Was he actually concerned about what Kristina would think of him? Or was he putting all of this pressure on himself? Was Kristina going to end the relationship because of his early ejaculation, or was he using his early ejaculation as an excuse to end the relationship?

Travis had a lot to work through over the next few months, particularly the guilt he felt from the loss of his first long-term relationship. Travis felt he had lost the love of his life, and the loss of the relationship resulted in the loss of maintaining ejaculatory control. Ultimately, when he met Kristina he had put her on a pedestal and given her so much praise because he was trying to recreate his lost relationship, hoping for a different outcome. A different outcome was unlikely to occur until Travis learned to let go of his guilt and have more self-worth. Kristina and Travis broke up after another two months because of his insecurities and inability to open up to her, but he continued to work on his issues in therapy, knowing they would resurface in a future relationship if he did not address them.

The reasons for experiencing early ejaculation are multi-faceted, but are typically resolvable with some self-introspection, hard work, and determination to create new boxes. When overcoming early ejaculation it is imperative to execute patience—the opposite of what your penis is doing during intimacy. Take a deep breath, do the exercises below, and take back control.

▪ EXERCISE ▪

One option to help with early ejaculation is to use a condom. A condom is a latex sheath, which fits snugly around the base of the penis. This sheath provides a barrier between the skin of the penis and what it is being inserted into (mouth, vagina, anus). Because the stimulation is not as direct, the sensitization is decreased. If this method works as desired, it also provides the person dealing with early ejaculation the confidence needed to prove that early ejaculation would *not* always occur. Since condoms do not have any adverse health affects (unless you are allergic to latex, in which case you could use lamb-skin or polyurethane condoms) there is no reason they can't be used long term. Please note: while this is a viable and cheap option, this solution is considered a quick fix, and will not address underlying emotional issues.

▪ EXERCISE ▪

Comparable to using a condom, but perhaps more pleasurable for both people, is to try using a penis ring, often referred to as a cock ring. Rings range in price, material, and function. You can purchase an affordable penis ring at your local drug store, an adult bookstore, or you can order a more technical one from an online retailer. While silicone-based rings tend to be more pliable and more comfortable, you can also purchase rings made of leather, nylon, rubber, glass, and even metal. Some have a vibrating option, which can make it easier to maintain an erection while also providing clitoral stimulation during vaginal intercourse. The ring is placed at the base of the penis during intimacy to help maintain an erection and offer additional pleasure. Once again, while this is a viable and affordable option, this solution is considered a quick fix, and will not address underlying emotional issues.

▪ EXERCISE ▪

Engage in mindfulness or a breathing exercise. These types of exercises are plentiful with a quick search on the computer. One of my favorites is an option you can do while lying down. The purpose of this exercise is to focus on what is happening to your body and the sensations you are feeling.

Once you are comfortable you should make sure your entire body is relaxed. Let your body get loose and as close to being a jellyfish as possible. Then, starting with your feet, tense them as much as you can for ten seconds. Relax. Next, tense your calves, and then relax. Tense your thighs, then relax. Move up your body, until you finally tense your neck, followed by your face.

Squeeze the muscles as hard as you can while you're flexing. Once each part of your body has engaged in the exercise, go back to being a jellyfish. If you still find it difficult to relax, do the exercise again. Be mindful throughout the process so you can reflect afterwards. The purpose of this exercise is to have control over what is happening to your body and to have the ability to bring it back to a relaxed state.

What was it like focusing on individual body parts? What happened to your breathing? Did it change at all? How did you feel after your entire body had an opportunity to tense itself?

▪ EXERCISE ▪

Grab some paper and a writing utensil. Find a comfortable place to sit and reflect about your body and your sexuality. Write down ten things you like about yourself. Consider your personality traits. Can you name ten physical traits you like about your body? What about your penis? What do you like about it? This exercise should only focus on positive things. If you feel comfortable, share your lists with a partner and discuss your responses. What would they add to your lists?

ERECTILE DYSFUNCTION

Erectile dysfunction is described as difficulty in obtaining or maintaining an erection during sexual activity. Obtaining and maintaining an erection is essential for most men to engage in sexual intimacy, to feel sexual pleasure, experience arousal, and achieve orgasm. When there is a loss of blood flow to the penis and erectile difficulties occur, most men panic. They may feel angry, confused, embarrassed, or anxious. While the experience of loss of erection is a fairly common one, it is often misunderstood and not discussed. It is estimated that over 50% of men in the United States will experience erectile dysfunction in their lifetime, a number topping between 18–33 million. Of these millions, one in four men under the age of 40 will seek treatment for erectile dysfunction, although they may not meet clinical requirements for a diagnosis.

As men age, erectile dysfunction issues become increasingly common with 40% of men over the age of 40, and 70% of men over the age of 70, experiencing it. Erectile dysfunction is more common in older men, affecting half of men over the age of 60. However, less than 10% of men under the age of 60 will experience this issue.

In addition to age, there are many things that can contribute to loss of erection, including alcohol consumption, anxiety, diabetes, an enlarged prostate, high blood pressure, high cholesterol, heart disease, lack of sleep, marijuana usage, being overweight, having a poor diet, a spinal cord injury, experiencing excess stress, tobacco usage, or a weak pelvic floor. Genetics also seem to be at play as some men can engage in an unhealthy lifestyle and have no trouble obtaining an erection, while other men drink a nightly beer and it affects blood flow to the penis.

The first thing anyone experiencing erectile dysfunction should do is schedule an appointment with a trusted urologist. It is imperative to rule out any medical concerns such as cardiac issues, since lack of blood flow can indicate serious health issues. However, a quick test to determine whether you are having medical or psychological issues is to answer the following questions: can you obtain and maintain an erection during masturbation? What about with a partner? Erectile dysfunction is typically a psychological issue when a man answers "yes" to the first question and "no" to the latter.

For most men experiencing erectile dysfunction due to psychological issues, there is an underlying anxiety issue. They may have anxiety about maintaining their erection and start thinking about it so much, putting pressure on themselves, they ultimately lose their erection. Other men are anxious about their relationship and begin to put an undue amount of pressure on their sexual performance. They subconsciously have a box filled with concerns the relationship will fail and their partner will leave them if they cannot perform sexually, and ultimately, they are unable to perform sexually.

Sometimes anxious thoughts will lead to self-fulfilling prophecies. Having a concern that you will lose your erection may mean that you will in fact lose your erection. Men may then enter into a vicious cycle of avoiding sexual encounters because they fear losing their erection. Their partner feels rejected and begins to think they aren't attractive anymore. When the couple does try to engage in sexual activity, there is so much pressure on it to be a positive experience that when it falls flat both withdraw and experience feelings of failure and rejection. If not treated, erectile dysfunction can be damaging to a relationship and to one's ego.

Case study: Emile and Peyton

I have met a lot of couples who have reached this place, with their relationship nearly at its breaking point. This was the case for Emile and Peyton, a gay couple in their late 30s. They had been dating for just over a year when Emile lost his erection during intimacy. He was immediately embarrassed and ended the sexual encounter. Feeling dejected, Peyton left the encounter thinking he had done something to upset Emile and fully took the blame for the loss of his erection. Rather than discussing what had happened, they each independently took full responsibility for the encounter. They also both hoped it was a fluke. Unfortunately, it happened again. Then again, and again. After several recurrences they began to avoid sex.

Three months passed before they discussed what was happening. Peyton was the one who brought it up to Emile, and he asked with tears in his eyes if Emile had found another man. He truly believed Emile could not maintain an erection in his presence because he was no longer attracted to Payton and did not love him anymore. While this conversation was very painful for them to have, it made Emile realize how this box filled with insecurity, guilt, and embarrassment had affected Peyton, whom he did love very much. It was during this honest discussion they decided to seek therapy so they could work through what was happening for both of them.

By the time they scheduled a session, the couple had not been sexually intimate for several months. They had become very good at avoiding sexual encounters. Neither had ended the relationship because they both thought the issue was their fault and had been trying to resolve it without intervention. They also thought the issue might eventually just "go away." Both Peyton and Emile were teary throughout that first session as they both absorbed the guilt they felt. They were also both relieved to learn that neither of them were to blame. They left their first session with a sense of hope they had not felt in months.

Like Peyton and Emile, many couples coping with erectile dysfunction choose to avoid intimacy altogether. Thanks to Hollywood and pornography, there is so much pressure to engage in intercourse that couples forget everything else on the sexual menu. However, there are many other intimate activities that couples can engage in other than intercourse, including the exercises at the end of the *Rekindling Desire, Sexual Scripts,* and *Kink* chapters.

Emile had a lot of underlying anxiety which was causing his erectile dysfunction. He was out of touch with his body and any time he and Peyton did try to be intimate, his mind began to wander. It was making ejaculatory control difficult because he was not present with himself or his partner. Anytime he did not obtain or maintain an erection, he would start to focus on this phenomenon. Sexual encounters that followed became so focused on whether he would be able to obtain or maintain an erection, it was all he was thinking about.

Emile then became one of those men who were engaging in a self-fulfilling prophecy. He was determined to have an erection, to be able to ejaculate with Peyton, to perform as a man is expected, and when he couldn't he felt like a failure, ridden with guilt and embarrassment. He was putting so much on himself pressure to perform and got so inside of his own head, and so out of touch with his own body, that it was almost inevitable he could not perform sexually. Ultimately, this self-fulfilling prophecy led to a vicious cycle of avoidance.

As you can see from Emile, many men will choose to stop the cycle by avoiding intimacy and sex altogether. The options feel like all or none, yet neither resolves the issue. Typically it makes it worse. How can one have control over their body if they are stuck inside their mind?

To begin having control over your mind and your body, you should begin doing the exercises discussed at the end of the *Early Ejaculation* chapter. The following exercises should also be implemented if you have difficulty obtaining or maintaining erections. Be patient with this process. Erectile difficulties do not develop overnight and cannot be resolved overnight either. If you do not see any improvement or success with the following exercises, consult a medical doctor for additional interventions.

■ EXERCISE ■

What do you have control over? Sometimes people feel like they do not have control over anything, which can feel defeating. When people feel they have no control over their erections, they can feel angry, disappointed, embarrassed, and guilty. Make a list of at least ten things you *do* have control over.

■ EXERCISE ■

It's time for a workout! In this exercise you will find and strengthen your pelvic floor muscles. You can find your pelvic floor by stopping the flow of urine while going to the bathroom.

Only do this once to identify the muscle, as doing this exercise while urinating can irritate the bladder. Once you've found your pelvic floor muscles, you can do this exercise while sitting or standing.

Begin by putting yourself in a relaxed state and then flex the muscle and hold for 10 seconds. Relax the muscle for 10 seconds. Flex. Relax. Flex. Relax. You can do this exercise for a few minutes several times a day, or do ten reps several times per day. Consider it a part of your workout routine. This is an internal muscle—being a runner, biker, swimmer, or weight-lifter does not mean you have a strong pelvic floor. Be intentional about this exercise. Notice if it is easier to relax your muscles, or if it easier to flex them. If you feel additional help would be beneficial, contact a local pelvic floor therapist in your area.

DELAYED EJACULATION

Delayed ejaculation is the least understood of all erectile issues among therapists and medical doctors, and occurs in less than 1% of men. While it is known in the medical community as delayed ejaculation it is also referred to as delayed orgasm, inhibited ejaculation, retarded ejaculation, or impaired ejaculation. Medical diagnosis requires that a man experience the inability to climax 75–100% of the time. While psychological stress is considered to be the number one cause of delayed ejaculation, other causes include sexual trauma, anxiety, depression, fear of impregnation, religious beliefs, use of anti-depressants or opiates, alcohol consumption, low levels of testosterone, thyroid issues, heart disease, or prior penile surgeries.

As with other erectile dysfunctions, it is important to consider what a person has control over and what they do not. For example, if a person is experiencing delayed ejaculation due to use of antidepressants, but the medication is preventing suicidal ideation, then they should stay on the medication and approach the issue from other angles. However, if a person is experiencing delayed ejaculation due to fear of impregnation, they can consider using contraceptives and work through their fears.

Case study: Ari and Sheila

This was the case for Ari and Sheila, who came to see me due to Ari's delayed ejaculation issues. Ari, a 36-year-old Jewish man, had been married to Sheila, 29, for two and a half years. He worked as a general contractor, was healthy and fit, and enjoyed bird watching. Sheila was a yoga instructor with a petite frame and big personality. They were both very likable, had an admirable relationship, and an active sex life. They enjoyed dressing up together and attending comic-cons, enjoying a bottle of red wine on the weekends, and spending time with their friends. The couple incorporated creativity and humor into their relationship. They got along well and were financially comfortable. If you weren't reading this chapter, you might begin to wonder why Ari and Sheila came to see me.

Ari explained in therapy that he was able to maintain an erection for a "very long time" during partnered sex, which allowed the couple to prolong their intimate experiences. For years they both enjoyed the fact that this offered them the time needed to focus on producing an orgasm for Sheila. The couple valued this while they were dating and early into their marriage, and didn't see it as an issue. But what was once convenient had turned into a problem now that they wanted to get pregnant. The more they discussed the idea of starting a family and began to try getting pregnant, the longer Ari noticed he was able to maintain an erection. The couple's former enthusiasm had turned to concern.

We began to discuss intimate details of the couple's sex life. The couple said their sexual routine included engaging in foreplay, but other than that it was sporadic. They enjoyed having sex in the morning and at night. They like to watch pornography and use toys, but said neither was necessary. They tried different sexual positions and engaged in role-play from time to time. No matter what they did, Ari could not bring himself to ejaculate. Ari did note that, "Sheila gets really wet, which I love, but sometimes she gets too wet, so we use a towel to wipe her."

Sheila blushed, and then turned to me and exclaimed, "I just think he's so attractive and I get turned on!" While this didn't seem like a big deal at first, Ari later noted that he doesn't use any kind of lubricant when masturbating and is always able to bring himself to climax. I immediately noted that Ari needed to change his masturbation routine to more closely match what partnered sex was like for him.

We also discussed Ari's upbringing, unpacking this box of history, as I had a feeling he had received some very specific messages about pregnancy as a teenager. I was right. Ari said his parents talked to him about sexuality twice, once to have a discussion about puberty, and once to tell him that he better not be having sex, but if he was he definitely better not get a girl pregnant. He said his father was a stern man with high expectations, and he was more afraid of the consequences from his father than the idea of being a teenage father. Regardless, the message was ingrained.

For over 20 years, Ari's mindset was to make sure he did not get a woman pregnant. Just because he was married, and the couple wanted children, didn't mean the message wasn't deeply rooted for Ari. It was time to do the hard work in therapy and start unwinding those messages while the couple engaged in sex and intimacy exercises at home. It took several months but eventually Ari was able to ejaculate inside of Sheila. Their openness and playful attitudes surely helped them achieve success faster. I was thrilled for them, and a year after we ended therapy I got an email with a picture of their baby boy.

As noted, delayed ejaculation is the most difficult and least understood of ejaculatory issues. There are many exercises to consider when dealing with this issue. It starts with letting go of control, letting yourself feel completely (in this situation it's okay to think with your other head), and relinquishing your anxieties and fears. While some of the exercises in the previous chapters on *Early Ejaculation* and *Erectile Dysfunction,* such as mindfulness and pelvic floor exercises, might help resolve delayed ejaculation, these additional exercises are pertinent.

■ EXERCISE ■

Take a blank piece of paper and draw a picture of your anxiety. What does it look like? Can you give your anxiety a name? It is easy to identify all the ways in which anxiety negatively impacts your life, but how does it positively influence your life? On the back of your picture, list all the positive things you get from anxiety.

■ EXERCISE ■

Journal the following questions by self-reflecting and writing your responses in a notebook. Once you've processed each question, decide if you'd like to discuss them with your partner. Recognizing, acknowledging, and validating these fears will help you to overcome them.

- Is the fear of getting someone pregnant preventing you from being able to ejaculate inside a partner?
- What messages did you receive about pregnancy growing up? Were they positive or negative? Were they viewed differently based on your age? Your relationship status?

- How have these messages influenced your sexual activity and use of contraceptives? Do you agree with these messages now? Why or why not?

- How do you feel about becoming a parent now? How do you feel about becoming a parent with your current partner? What are you most afraid of?

▪ EXERCISE ▪

One method that Ari and Sheila found helpful was the stuff-it method. Ari would masturbate, almost to the point of orgasm, and then insert his penis inside of Sheila just before he was about to ejaculate. Not only did this instill confidence in him so he could ejaculate inside of Sheila, it also helped his body learn to ejaculate to new sensations, including Sheila's natural vaginal lubrication.

To try the stuff-it method yourself, begin by engaging in partner play. You can engage in sexual activities you both have tried and enjoy doing, or you can try something new. When you are ready, begin to masturbate yourself. If you feel comfortable, you can have your partner assist by massaging your testicles or anus. Once you find that you are close to having an orgasm, exercise ejaculatory control, and insert, or "stuff," your penis inside of your partner. This method helps to overcome the anxiety and fear associated with ejaculating inside of a partner and proves to yourself that you can.

VAGINAL AND VULVAR PAIN

While many things can be normalized with regard to sexuality, vaginal and vulvar pain are not something that should be happening. Unfortunately, these issues are more common than discussed and the women experiencing them are often ignored or not believed by their doctors. Being ignored by a medical professional you've placed your trust in leads to filling up a box with guilt, shame, loneliness, and anxiety.

Before discussing the different types of pain, let's be clear about the anatomy we are discussing. If you happen to have a vagina, go grab a mirror, lie down, spread your legs apart, and take a peek. What you see, all of the external features, are called the vulva. We often mistakenly refer to all of these external parts as the vagina but we are actually referring to the vulva. The vagina is the muscular tube located inside the body. It is about 4–6 inches in length and expands up to 200% when sexually aroused. It is where a person might insert a tampon, a penis, fingers, or a sex toy. Menstrual blood, or a baby, comes out of the vagina.

The images below, from *Vaginas and Periods 101: A Pop-Up Book* will give you a clearer idea of external versus internal anatomy.

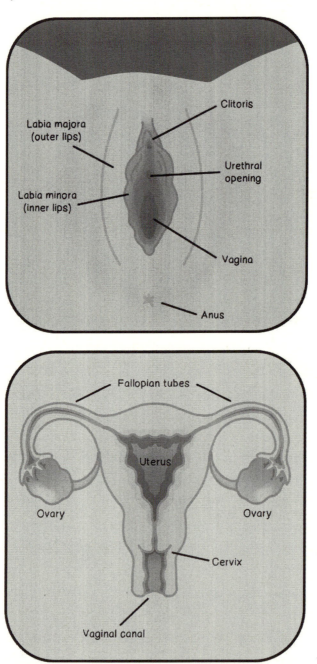

Now that we've covered the basics, let's talk about vulvar and vaginal pain. There are several types of genital pain that women may experience. The most common one is known as vulvodynia, the experience of chronic and spontaneous vulvar pain. Despite this being the most common pain disorder experienced by women, "there is no single cause of vulvodynia" (Goldstein, 2011, p. 69). Since the root cause is often unobtainable, "you're likely to be diagnosed with vulvodynia when your doctor can't find anything else wrong with you, but you still have pain in your vulvar area" (Goldstein, 2011, p. 66).

Less common is vestibulodynia, which is also referred to by the International Society for Sexual Medicine as "provoked vestibulodynia." This is pain experienced at the entrance of the vagina from light touch and hypersensitivity, when a person reacts strongly to physical stimuli. The pain may occur during sexual activities but irritation could also be caused from something as mundane as the rubbing of clothing on the vulva. This is *not* an internal pain within the vagina, so intercourse may still be an option. However, the inflammation at the opening of the vagina may be so intense that penetration is not possible. Various research studies show that as many as 16% of women may suffer from vestibulodynia.

Another type of pain experienced by women is genito-pelvic pain, also known as "penetration disorder." It affects about 15% of women in North America and refers to the fear of vaginal penetration during intercourse. Women with penetration disorder may experience marked pain during intercourse or the tensing or tightening of the pelvic floor muscles, which may prevent them from having intercourse altogether. This phenomenon is often referred to as dyspareunia, which refers to difficult or painful intercourse.

Finally, vaginismus is the most common vulvar or vaginal pain disorder. It is more easily diagnosed by a doctor, and is experienced by 1 in 500 women. Vaginismus is vaginal tightness that causes discomfort, burning, pain, penetration problems, or the complete inability to have intercourse. The vaginal tightness occurs due to the tightening of the vaginal muscles. "When these muscles are tight, less blood flows through them, providing less oxygen to cells and resulting in a build of lactic acid" (Goldstein, 2011, p. 88). It is the acid that is causing the burning sensation inside the vagina. These women are unlikely to be able to insert tampons as well.

In addition to the vaginal and vulvar conditions discussed, pain may develop after childbirth. Postpartum intercourse may hurt for a variety of reasons including tearing during childbirth, scar tissue, damage to the tailbone during delivery, pudendal nerve damage, and hormonal changes. Women who breastfeed after childbirth are likely to experience atrophy or dryness because the vaginal tissue naturally thins. This often resolves itself once the mother has finished breastfeeding her child. Lubricant can also help alleviate the problem. While postpartum pain is common, there are preventative strategies to utilize while pregnant which are outlined more specifically in the *Pregnancy and Sex* chapter.

As you have read through all of the types of disorders in this chapter, the most common *symptom* of vulvar and vaginal disorders is pain. Depending on the disorder, other symptoms include tightening of the pelvic floor muscles, vaginal dryness, and burning sensations. Seeking a doctor immediately is the first step to addressing these issues and resolving the pain. While some of the disorders, such as vulvodynia, have no known cause, others occur due to infection or nerve damage. Causes for pain range drastically but include anxiety, childbirth, cysts, endometriosis, menopause, pelvic inflammatory disease, sexually transmitted infections or diseases, sexual trauma, vaginal dryness, and other vaginal infections. Sometimes making a diagnosis is easy, but other times, such as with vulvodynia, it can be complicated and take a long time for a doctor to make a diagnosis.

While dealing with vulvar and vaginal pain is emotionally exhausting and physically painful, there are a variety of treatment options available for sufferers. Personally, I see a lot of progress as a therapist by helping clients discuss the pain they are feeling, the anxiety they are experiencing, and discussing alternative ways to create intimacy. Oftentimes these clients also consult with a doctor or pelvic floor therapist while they are working through emotional stress in therapy.

Medical interventions such as a topical medication like Lidocaine, or an injection such as Botox, may help women overcome pain. Doctors or physical therapists may also help stretch the pelvic floor muscles using dilators. Sometimes doctors see success by prescribing an antidepressant, which serves to "reduce the signals traveling through the nerves of the central nervous system (the spinal cord and brain), thus reducing the pain" (Goldstein, 2011, p. 92). Diet and herbal remedies, acupuncture, a chiropractor, and hypnosis are less traditional options, which may also provide pain relief for some people. It is best to consult with a professional before deciding how to proceed so you can determine what is causing the pain, prevent inflammation, and find relief.

Case study: Isha and Kazi

Sometimes the case of vaginal or vulvar pain is medical, sometimes it is emotional, but most of the time it is a combination of the two. In the case of Isha, a 24-year-old Muslim-African refugee, it was both. She and her spouse, Kazi, 34, had been living in the United States for over ten years. In addition to the stress of the move, they were new parents to their first child, a four-month-old daughter named Habiba.

Since the birth of Habiba, the couple had been unable to have intercourse at all due to the vulvar pain Isha was experiencing. During a routine exam, her physician couldn't find anything wrong, and told her she was healing well post-partum. It made Isha feel like she was making up the pain, and it had begun to cause friction between her and Kazi.

"Why can't she have sex? The doctor sees nothing wrong," Kazi complained. He was getting frustrated and felt conflicted about their doctor's professional expertise and his wife's firsthand experience. He continued, "She starts to cry if we try to have sex. I just don't understand how she can cry but the doctor finds nothing. Do you even still love me?" Kazi's own self-esteem was beginning to wane under the weight of the sexual tension that had been created. He doubted himself because he couldn't please his wife. He doubted the doctor who didn't find any clear cause of the pain. And he doubted Isha was telling him the truth. He felt betrayed and was not sure how to process the conflicting information he was receiving.

Isha wept while Kazi expressed himself. Finally she spoke, her voice unwavering as if she hadn't just been crying. "I am a lot of things, Kazi. I am a wife, a mother, a daughter, a friend, and I *am* in pain. But I am *not* a liar." We spent several sessions validating both of their experiences. Kazi had begun to take his frustrations out on his wife, rather than using the momentum to support her and learn to love her and be intimate in other ways. I instructed the couple to stop trying to have sex, since it was leading to a poor experience, resentment, and lack of trust for both of them. This was a box we needed to throw away so we could then focus on filling up a new one.

We discussed other ways they could be physically intimate, utilizing exercises from prior chapters, and the couple learned to express love and intimacy in new ways. Isha spent time learning to relax, associating Kazi's touch with positive feelings. This helped her to trust him and feel less anxious so her body did not tense when he went to hug her. Time was also spent helping her to trust herself again. Hearing from her doctor there was nothing wrong and hearing the distrust from Kazi, Isha began to doubt herself. She didn't know how to trust her body anymore. Her genitals, which had once provided sexual release and pleasure, had betrayed her. Being able to relieve her anxieties and relax allowed Isha to be more present in her own body. Eventually she stopped associating touch with pain.

In addition to therapy, Isha was referred to a doctor who specialized in vulvodynia. This specialized doctor did find that Isha had some scar tissue built-up from childbirth, as well as an infection. She was given medication to clear up the infection and was taught how to do perineal massage to loosen up the scar tissue. This doctor helped reassure Isha there was a cause for her pain and validated her experience. The medical explanation also helped Kazi begin to understand what his wife was experiencing. They were able to discuss what the doctor said in sessions as they continued to process their own feelings and rebuild the trust between them.

It took several months for the couple to relearn touch and reestablish trust, but talking through their issues and getting validation and help from professionals helped them to communicate and love in new ways. With the relief from the pain, Isha's confidence in her genitals was rebuilt. The couple maintained a healthy sex life, pain free, for another six months until they decided to have a second child. They had some fears they would experience the same trauma of sexual pain, but they also felt confident in the skills they had learned to navigate it.

When pain is involved, it is important for couples to stop having sexual intercourse while working through the other issues the pain has caused. Women need to learn to trust themselves, even when their doctors can't find a cause. They need their partners to trust them and not take sexual rejection personally. You're pain is not normal, but it is real.

■ EXERCISE ■

Once you've made a doctor appointment and addressed any kind of medical issues you may be experiencing, you can begin focusing on your anxiety and learn to trust your genitals. Before you answer these questions and do this exercise, find a quiet place to sit or lay down. Close your eyes and let your body sink in as you relax. If you have a difficult time relaxing, take several deep breaths to help calm your body and your mind. Once you've centered yourself, consider journaling through this exercise.

How well do you know your body? Perhaps you once knew it quite well, but since the pain started you aren't sure how to trust it anymore. What did you trust about your body that you don't trust anymore? What do you still trust about your body? What is something you would change about your body? What do you love about your body?

Now, recall a time when you had a gut reaction to something. What happened? What was your body telling you? Where did you feel it in your body? Was it in your bones? Your stomach? Did it feel fluttery or did your body tense up? Was it a good hunch you were feeling? A bad one? How did it feel to follow your instincts?

Consider a time when you had a gut reaction that you ignored. What was your body telling you on this occasion? Why did you ignore it? How did it feel to ignore that feeling?

Now, think about a problem or issue you are currently dealing with. It could be an issue you are dealing with at work or home. Sit for a few minutes and close your eyes while you think about the problem. Pay attention to what is happening to your body.

What is your body telling you about this problem? Is it something that makes you feel nervous? Scared? Angry? Anxious? If you notice your body is starting to tense, take a moment to do some deep breathing again. Once you've let yourself calm down and relax, does the problem seem as overwhelming as it did a few minutes ago? What changed in your body? Consider how you might handle the problem differently based on how your body is feeling right now.

Keep doing this exercise to practice slowing down your thoughts as you notice what is happening to your body. Take more time to listen to your body. Feed it what it needs. Trust your instincts. Know that relaxing *will* help relieve your tension and anxiety. As the anxiety starts to wane and you become more relaxed, you will start to trust the vaginal or vulvar pain you are experiencing. Why are you experiencing this pain?

Acknowledge that the pain is real but know that it will start to wane as well. Be patient with yourself and your body. Trust that the pain you are experiencing is your body's way of protecting you. Ignoring that pain and anxiety will only exacerbate it. Don't lose trust in yourself. Believe in yourself. Believe in your body.

In addition to this exercise, you should do the breathing exercise in the *Early Ejaculation* chapter, begin pelvic floor exercises discussed in the *Erectile Dysfunction* chapter, and engage in non-demand touch exercises with your partner as outlined in the chapter on *Low Libido*. Make sure you are also communicating with your partner about your experience so they can validate it, while you also validate their experience using the Pancake Talk from the *Fantasy* chapter!

106

POLYAMORY, OPEN RELATIONSHIPS, AND SWINGING

There are a variety of relationship dynamics that people can choose from. Most people are familiar with monogamy and committing romantically and sexually to one person. You may be reading this chapter because you are interested in pursuing ethical non-monogamy, or just want to learn more about different types of relationships. Ethical non-monogamy means that all people involved are consenting and agreeing to an arrangement. This chapter will explore the idea of ethical non-monogamous relationship models including polyamory, open relationships, and swinging.

Polyamory is a progressive relationship concept that pushes the boundaries of monogamy. It's a relationship theory that challenges the idea that one person can meet all of our needs, and that loving more than one person allows for the fulfillment and growth we need as people. Polyamory acknowledges both the complexities of people and relationships themselves. It is the idea of loving more than one person and maintaining a relationship with them.

Perhaps the most important factor is that it is rooted in communication, honesty, and transparency. Polyamory is a relationship approach where the people involved are engaged in a loving and respectful relationship. A former client referred to the polyamorous dynamic as a "perfect bubble" that she was in, along with her partners.

The boundaries and relationship dynamics within polyamory vary drastically. For example, Karen may be in a relationship with Dean. Then Karen meets Brad and they fall in love. Perhaps Dean and Brad both feel fulfilled by Karen, making their relationship a V (with Karen at the center). Maybe Karen is with Dean and Brad, and Dean and Brad also have another partner. Maybe it's the same partner making it a quad, maybe it isn't. As you can see, polyamory could lead to a long relationship chain or it could stop and start with Karen. This could also change over time as each individual's relationship needs change. Break-ups may be inevitable, children may be born, or infidelity could occur.

Some polyamorous relationship dynamics favor the initial relationship as the "primary" relationship. That means that Karen and Dean are considered to be in a primary relationship. There are many things that constitute a primary relationship, including longevity of the relationship, living together, sharing finances, or having children. The couple will make relationship agreements, including verbal or written contracts, before dating other people.

When Karen enters into a relationship with Brad, this is called a "secondary" relationship. It has been deemed a secondary relationship because Karen and Brad might not spend every night together or share finances, but they do offer one another emotional support. However, it's also possible that Karen and

Brad might have a tertiary relationship, wherein they provide one another emotional support and are intimate, but they do not see one another consistently and their time spent together is erratic. In addition, Dean might decide Karen is enough for him, although Karen dates others, and they now have a mono-poly relationship. Many people also choose to ditch the definitions and consider all partners equally important, rather than engaging in a hierarchy. Confused yet?

While it can be complicated, when polyamory works well, it is because people have openly agreed to this relationship model. Often a couple will come into my office because one of them has committed infidelity, then discovers the word polyamory, and uses it as a reason for the behavior, urging their partner to let them continue the affair with their blessing and consent, newly labeled as polyamory. Situations that start with infidelity need to first address the issues within the relationship before stepping outside of those confines.

When polyamory works, it is because the couple has agreed to be polyamorous in the first place. It must start from a place of openness that is based on mutual trust. It is plausible that a person really has discovered the meaning of polyamory and identifies with it after an affair, but they are at an unfair vantage point while their partner processes the concept. It is best for the affair to end while the couple decides if this relationship model is something they are *both* open to experiencing, taking time to reestablish trust.

Case study: Jarryd and Eve

A young couple in their late 20s, Jarryd and Eve had been dating and cohabitating for three years and had several room-mates over the years. They came to see me after Eve shared she had been having an affair with their current roommate for the last two months. Jarryd was hurt by the news and unsure how to process it all. He felt deceived by Eve and by their roommate Matt, whom he had considered a friend. However, Jarryd also expressed he loved Eve and wanted to figure out how to make this work. Eve expressed regret and guilt for the infidelity. "I never meant to hurt you," she professed through tears to Jarryd repeatedly in therapy. Despite feeling remorse for hurting Jarryd, she had also fallen in love with Matt.

While trying to sort through her own feelings, Eve said she discovered the word polyamory on the Internet. "I read about it and realized, that's me! Thinking back on my life, I've always been a serial monogamous dater. I always had someone else lined up before ending a relationship. I also realized that when I met someone new, I felt like I had to break up with the other person because it was never an option to be with both. I could have saved myself and others a lot of heartache if I had been introduced to polyamory sooner," she confided.

Jarryd said he was not hurt by the idea of polyamory; he was hurt that Eve had cheated on him. Jarryd felt he would have been more open to the idea of polyamory if Eve and Matt had not betrayed his trust. Still, Jarryd was invested in the relationship and was open to trying this dynamic for the sake of Eve. "I'm not going to put pressure on her to end things with Matt. She's in love with him. That's not going to work in my favor. I want her to sort this out, and I'm going to be here for her while she does that. I want this to work and I want to trust my partner and my friend again," Jarryd humbly communicated.

Jarryd engaged in some individual sessions to process his box of emotions during this too. He admitted he was actually open to the idea of polyamory but felt "blind-sided" by Eve's confession, as well as the betrayal from her and Matt. This was making it difficult for him to rebuild trust.

Their couples sessions focused on rebuilding this trust and discussing how Eve could establish boundaries that respected the needs of everyone. Eventually Matt came to therapy as well, and the trio discussed all of their unspoken feelings. Matt admitted he felt "jealous" of Eve's commitment to Jarryd. He knew Eve was not going to leave Jarryd to be with him, which was both understandable and frustrating for him. It was the first time Jarryd and Matt had an open discussion about everything that was happening under the roof they all shared. The conversation was emotional and difficult, but it might have been the first time that honesty and transparency were truly present.

To move forward in this relationship dynamic, they were asked to sit down, engage in the Pancake Talk from the *Fantasy* chapter, and establish boundaries so they all felt respected. They were also asked to individually consider what kind of self-care they each needed during this process.

Ultimately, Jarryd and Eve worked things out. Within a year, they even got pregnant and had a baby together. Upon finding out she was pregnant, and reassuring Jarryd the baby was his, she decided to end the relationship with Matt and focus on her growing family. In retrospect, Eve noted, "I went about starting a relationship with Matt all wrong. I should have communicated more with Jarryd when I was feeling unhappy. I still think polyamory is the relationship dynamic for me, but I want to focus on my family right now. If someone else enters my life, I think Jarryd and I will be able to address it the right way next time."

By definition, open relationships are different than polyamorous ones. Open relationships refer to couples who have agreed to have sex with other people outside of the relationship. The agreement is limited to sexual acts without an emotional investment. The arrangement may vary drastically within relationships though. Couples may want to know everything about another person's sexual partners, or they may want to know nothing. Some people have a "zip code rule" where it is okay to have sex with someone else but only when traveling. Others want to ensure emotional attachments don't occur, so they request that their partner limit sexual encounters to one-night-stands. It may also be that only one person has an interest in an open relationship but receives permission and support from their partner. Sometimes a person experiencing illness or recurrent pain encourages their partner to have sex with others since it is not something they feel they can provide, but couples may not feel it is an issue worthy splitting ways. However people decide to navigate an open relationship, it can become deeply personal and intricate from couple to couple.

Case study: Johanah and Erik

When Johanah and Erik came to their first appointment, they jumped right in. The retired couple had been married for nearly 40 years and had two grown children. Their love and affection for one another was apparent as they completed each other's sentences and held hands in sessions. Erik had been experiencing erectile dysfunction for nearly five years now after having prostate cancer. The couple shared that they engaged in intimacy and loved to cuddle, but were unable to have vaginal intercourse.

Erik felt guilty for being unable to sexually perform and expressed to Johanah that it would be okay with him if she wanted to find another man to have sex with. "I thought the whole thing was ridiculous," she said with a small laugh.

Admittedly, Erik thought it was ridiculous at first too, and had said it only in jest. The more he thought about it though, the more he thought it might just be the answer to their problems. The couple shared they had discussed it at length, and both agreed it would be a way to enhance their intimacy and sexual relationship.

They decided together to recycle the concept of monogamy and open a new box with this relationship concept.

Johanah had warmed up to the idea that having sex with another man would be pleasurable, and she was open to sharing her encounters with Erik so he could vicariously be part of the experience as well. This was a well-adjusted couple who just wanted some direction to start opening up their relationship.

Johanah and Erik were encouraged to discuss their personal boundaries. They created a relationship agreement, found at the end of this chapter, and said it helped them think of boundaries they would not have otherwise considered. They also read two books together about non-monogamy, *The Ethical Slut* and *Opening Up*. While they didn't feel everything they read was applicable to their situation, it encouraged them to have thoughtful conversations about ethical non-monogamy. As often happens, unexpected feelings arose for Johanah and Erik. While they felt things were manageable and were able to discuss them, they did so in therapy so they could have a sounding board. The couple felt prepared for exploring an open relationship, but they wanted to ensure they handled it with grace. And they did.

Case study: Alex and Safairra

Another relationship model that people engage in is swinging. The most basic idea is that couples sexually swap partners with another couple. Swinging parties are a trendy and accessible way to meet other couples without any obligation to engage in a relationship. Single women are often invited and welcome at these parties, so couples can engage in a threesome, but single men have been considered predatory in the swinging scene and are usually not invited alone.

For Alex and Safairra, a couple in their mid-forties, getting involved in swinging was not the problem. They had been intermittently involved in the swinging scene for the last 15 years. Safairra worked for a consulting company and Alex had pursued a second career as a high school English teacher after working as a lawyer for over a decade. They had no children due to infertility issues. They made up for the loss through their adventurous lifestyle, and had enjoyed many thrills from skydiving to hiking through the Brazilian rainforest. The couple had also engaged in a thrilling sex life and had enjoyed many experiences together including taking a rope-and-bondage class together.

Alex shared that he was "very open-minded" and identified as bisexual. He was genuinely open to trying any sexual experience at least once. While Alex's *laissez faire* attitude was what Safairra loved about him, she said she did not want to keep engaging in the swinging lifestyle.

Alex was obviously upset and confused by this sentiment. "You always seem to have a good time when we do it." She said she had done it for the past 15 years because it made Alex happy, but it conflicted with her values. When pressed, Safairra could not articulate what value she was referring to. They had this conversation at least a dozen times on their own before deciding to set up a therapy appointment.

Safairra felt if swinging was that important to Alex then he should leave her. Offering her reassurance, Alex shared, "I don't want to do it with someone else. It's a valuable experience because I get to do it with you."

She reiterated it just did not align with her values and she was "done with swinging." In therapy, Safairra was again asked about the box of values she was referring to and was encouraged to expand on them. She got flustered at the question, unable to elaborate, and said, "It's just not right, him being with another woman in front of me." The couple discussed this in-depth as Safairra contradicted herself and seemed unsure of what her values were. Safairra was given space and freedom within therapy to consider how she had filled a box with values, and as she unpacked them, to discuss what they meant to her personally and within her marriage.

It took several sessions before Safairra had unpacked this box and could express her views before she realized her insecurities had nothing to do with her value system but stemmed from her own issues with infertility. Safairra recognized that she had a fear of Alex getting another woman pregnant, as well as feelings of jealousy towards women that shared they were mothers themselves. These feelings began to cheapen the experience of swinging for her. Alex and Safairra spent time discussing and processing these feelings, and created a relationship contract, as they discussed how to navigate moving forward to maintain a healthy and exciting sex life.

The crossover between polyamory, open relationships, and swinging is open communication and honesty. Oftentimes people just need some basic education to be able to have this kind of open communication and discuss their boundaries, just like in monogamous relationships. Creating a relationship contract helps many people articulate these boundaries. Couples may have an idea of what they want to explore in their relationship and just need some assistance to ensure they navigate it in a healthy manner. Another key factor is that rules and boundaries can, and do, change. Relationships that are open may later become closed, and vice versa. Deciding if opening up your relationship is for you goes back to communicating with your partner and being in touch with your own sexual self.

■ EXERCISE ■

Now that you've finished this chapter, you may be wondering if a non-monogamous relationship is something you want to explore. There's a lot to think about to decide if opening up your relationship is right for you and your partner. Ask yourself the following questions:

1. What is appealing to me about a monogamous relationship?

2. What is appealing to me about an open/polyamorous relationship?

3. What do you want out of a romantic relationship?

4. Is my current relationship happy, stable, and fulfilling?

5. Am I a jealous person?

6. Does the thought of having to structure my time for multiple partners sound manageable or stressful?

7. Am I a good communicator?

8. Is my partner a good communicator?

9. Would opening up my relationship bring fulfillment or stress? How would I manage these emotions?

10. Does swinging with my partner sound like a fun connecting experience, or would it invoke feelings of jealousy and insecurity?

After you have given these questions a lot of thought, decide if you would like to share your thoughts with your partner, even if your decision is to continue a monogamous relationship. Having similar values and navigating difficult conversations with your partner will create trust and connection.

■ EXERCISE ■

So you've decided you want to open up your relationship—you just aren't sure how. Begin by doing your research. Many cities have polyamorous communities and swinging parties that are easily accessible with a quick Internet search. Even if you don't live in a large city, consider joining a social media support group. Online support groups often share experiences and offer tips. You could also create an online dating profile at a site that supports non-monogamy, such as FetLife, known for its support of the kink community. Many couples will even create a profile together to help maintain transparency.

■ EXERCISE ■

Create a relationship agreement. This is a good starting place to establish the boundaries within your relationship *before* adding another relationship to the mix. Revisit the contract every few weeks or months initially. It is hard to predict exactly what will happen in polyamorous or open relationships, because humans are unpredictable. A relationship agreement offers a road map as a starting place to navigate unexpected things. It also ensures that polyamory, an open relationship, or swinging start from a place of communication and transparency. As one client said, having a contract "was a nice exercise," however "a few months into it we quickly decided that setting up strict rules and guidelines didn't work for us. We dwindled it down to the Golden Rule, but it was a helpful place to start!" The following example is your starting place.

Relationship Agreement

With the goal of transparency, communication, honesty, and a loving relationship, _____ and _____ have discussed and agreed upon the following ground rules for their relationship, dated _____. This agreement shall be reviewed three months from today and shall be updated/edited/renegotiated at this time if deemed necessary. We understand that a written agreement cannot account for all situations, but we

enter into the following with the intent to support one another
and cause no harm.

We hereby define our relationship as_____
which means: _____

_____

_____

1. We have discussed and identified the following emotional
needs to be met: _____

_____

_____

_____

2. We have discussed and identified that the following physical
needs to be met: _____

_____

_____

_____

3. We have agreed to the following rules about sexual contact
with others: _____

_____

_____

_____

4. We have agreed to share the following with each other
about emotional/intimate/sexual experiences with other
people: _____

_____

_____

_____

5. We have agreed the following rules shall not be broken:___

_____

_____

_____

_____

6. We have agreed the following shall only occur with one another: _____

_____

_____

_____

7. In the event of jealousy, we agree to address it in the following way: _____

_____

_____

_____

8. In the event of an STI, STD, or unplanned pregnancy we agree to: _____

_____

_____

_____

9. I _____ would like to personally note the following: _____

_____

_____

_____

10. I _____ would like to personally note

the following: _____

_____

_____

_____

11. In order to maintain transparency and honesty, we agree

to: _____

_____

_____

_____

12. If a rule is broken, or we feel disrespected, we agree to:

_____

_____

_____

_____

13. Additional notes and amendments:_____

_____

_____

_____

_____

Our intention in the creation of this document is to ensure the
quality and character of our relationship. We have discussed
and agreed to everything that is contained within this document. We are aware that we cannot plan for every circum-
stance but agree to discuss situations as they arise so that we
can handle them with integrity. If at any time, this document

no longer serves its written purpose, we agree to change it accordingly.

Signed _____

Date _____

Signed _____

Date _____

JEALOUSY

The *Merriam-Webster Dictionary* defines the concept of jealousy as being, "hostile toward a rival or one believed to enjoy an advantage." It is synonymous with *envy* and typically associated with phrases like, *green with envy*. The saying is actually poetic, originating from Shakespeare's play *Othello* in 1622. "O, beware, my lord, of jealousy; it is the green-eyed monster which doth mock the meat it feeds on," says the protagonist Iago, when he accuses another character of infidelity.

While experiencing feelings of jealousy is both normal and common, it is an uncomfortable emotion. Oftentimes, we don't know how to handle feelings of jealousy and it comes out in unpleasant ways. Jealousy can make us hostile, irrational, angry, and judgmental. It may be an emotion that covers up what we are actually feeling, such as hurt or defeat, as we experience a lack of self-confidence in ourselves. Jealousy may also arise when a situation is out of our control and we don't know what else to do but feel envy towards someone else.

Within the context of relationships, people may experience feelings of jealousy for a variety of reasons. Feelings of jealousy often arise for people in non-monogamous relationships. Being cheated on will elicit feelings of jealousy. The birth of a child, and the additional attention warranted towards a newborn, may cause jealousy. Others feel jealous when a partner is making more money in the relationship, or when one person's career is doing better than your own.

Sometimes we don't understand why we are experiencing feelings of jealousy. Why feel jealous when your partner is successful? It is likely a reflection that we do not feel as successful as we want to, but shouldn't we be happy for our partner? Rationally, don't we understand that a new baby is going to require more time and attention from a partner? Opening up this box and reflecting about why you are experiencing feelings of jealousy can help, but it's also important to acknowledge that this feeling isn't always rational.

Case study: Suzanne and Randy

Because jealousy isn't always a rational emotion, people don't always know how to unpack and recycle this box. This was the case for Suzanne and Randy. Suzanne was a 39-year-old financial analyst and Randy was a 42-year-old fireman. They had been married for 12 years and had no children due to infertility issues. They had found that being a DINK (double income, no kids) couple had its advantages and they found other ways to fulfill their lives, such as traveling, rock climbing, and running marathons together.

Recently, the couple had decided to spice up their sex life by engaging in swinging. "It was actually Suzy's idea," Randy shared, although he was very open to exploring it. "I mean, isn't it every guy's dream to have a threesome?" he joked.

The couple felt they had navigated the situation well so far. After reading *Opening Up* by Tristan Taormino, they had a better idea of what they should expect. The book had generated a lot of discussion between them and they felt comfortable taking the next step. This led them to meeting other couples who engaged in swinging so they could learn more about the "scene." Through this process they had learned some things about themselves and one another, and discussed boundaries they felt were important. They had made new friends and had new lovers.

One thing the couple was not able to plan for was feelings of jealousy that arose. "We thought that setting guidelines and talking about our boundaries would eliminate any of that," Suzanne explained.

Randy sheepishly looked up. "It's my fault," he said. Suzanne comforted Randy and reassured him they were okay. I pushed for them to elaborate on what had happened.

They shared they had three different sexual experiences with other couples. The first two went really well and there were no issues. On the third occasion, Randy shared he wasn't as into the woman, who was more interested in being a spectator anyway. He tried to watch Suzanne and the woman's husband have sex, but as he did he started to feel jealous. "I wanted to have sex with Suzanne, or at least be a part of it. I wasn't sure how to get involved without seeming possessive or controlling. And I didn't want to interrupt. It was awkward at best," he confided.

Suzanne took his hand and again offered him reassurance. I also offered validation, and we began to discuss why Randy was feeling jealous and how to navigate this situation. Randy had realized that swinging and swapping were quite different from the fantasy he'd had of a threesome. We discussed setting realistic expectations to curb his jealousy, and utilized the exercises at the end of this chapter. We also discussed what the couple could do next time they were in a situation with another couple but ultimately wanted to have sex with each another. They talked about how to say something and advocate for themselves and one another in a way that felt comfortable, but not possessive. "We just didn't realize we should even have this conversation," Suzanne said.

Randy concurred, then elaborated, "I never saw myself as the jealous type. It makes me feel really... insecure."

Once again, Suzanne validated his feelings and reassured him that what he was feeling was normal. She even laughed, saying, "I think *I'd* be jealous if *you* weren't a little bit jealous."

They decided to continue with therapy for a few months so they could discuss their experiences and continue to deal with them appropriately as new situations came up. The couple also utilized *The Jealousy Workbook* by Kathy Labriola to help them navigate situations as they arose. They noted how helpful it was to be forced to examine their own feelings of jealousy in ways they didn't realize it was affecting them.

Case study: Mario and Carolyn

While feelings of jealousy are common to experience when opening up a relationship, or when instances of infidelity occur, sometimes they occur in less traditional or obvious ways. I worked with a young couple who experienced unwanted feelings of jealousy after having a baby. Mario and Carolyn were a young couple in their mid-20s. Mario was a journalist and they met when he was writing an article for the paper and did an interview with Carolyn. They had their first baby, Isabella, eight months ago and found they had become distant, angry, and resentful towards each another over the last few months.

Their first session was emotional. They both cried. Mario wanted the session to be productive, though, so he sat up straight, took a deep breath, and began. "I can't believe I'm saying this, but I'm—I'm jealous. Ever since we had Isabella, Carolyn doesn't have time for me. I thought having a baby would be fulfilling, but it feels like the opposite."

Carolyn stopped crying abruptly. *"That's* why you've pulled away from me? You're jealous of a *baby?"* She was both hurt and aghast at what Mario was confessing. "All these months I thought you weren't attracted to me anymore," she said, flabbergasted, and began to cry again.

Immediately Mario felt embarrassed, both at how he felt and for his lack of communication. He reassured Carolyn he was immensely attracted to her. He just felt he couldn't "compete" with Isabella. "Of course, rationally, I *know* she's a baby. Babies have a lot of needs and Carolyn is such a fantastic mother. I feel like a horrible father. I've become jealous and resentful. Who resents their own child like this?" he said through his own tears of shame.

As we began working together, there was a big box to unpack from Mario's upbringing. Mario had grown up in a home with nine other siblings so he was always fighting for attention. Growing up, he had tried getting into trouble to get more attention, getting good grades to get more attention, and playing competitive sports to get more attention. At home, he found nothing worked and he began to feel he wasn't worthy of the attention he craved.

Mario finally found solace in his high school journalism class through Mr. Jones, his teacher. Mr. Jones saw Mario's talent as a writer. He became a mentor for Mario, believed in his abilities, and encouraged him to go to college and become a journalist. Mario didn't experience this kind of attention again until he met Carolyn.

After Isabella was born, his own childhood triggered him, and he remembered that nothing he could do would ever win his parents' attention, so how could he possibly win Carolyn's?

Carolyn was able to hold space for him as he processed his childhood aloud for the first time. When he opened up, he also began to take responsibility for the hurt he had caused Carolyn over the last few months since his anger, resentment, and withdrawal had affected their relationship. "Jealousy is real," Mario realized. "It's all I experienced growing up. I just never thought I'd have it towards my own child."

As the couple began to move back towards one another, I offered another revelation for Mario about being a parent. "You also get attention from your daughter." It clicked and Mario exclaimed, "I've been too wrapped up in myself to realize all of the attention I am getting from my child. I was so focused and jealous of the attention she was taking *away* from me, it didn't occur to me all of the attention I get *from* her." This simple but pertinent reframe helped Mario recycle a box. He started to invest in his marriage and as a father in ways he didn't realize were possible for him. The wounds of his childhood began to heal, and as the jealousy melted away, his heart began to swell.

Again, it is normal to experience feelings of jealousy from time to time. It is how we choose to cope with those feelings that ultimately affects both others and ourselves. Continue with the exercises below the next time you are face-to-face with the green-eyed monster!

■ EXERCISE ■

How can you navigate feelings of jealousy? Grab some paper and journal for this exercise. Can you recall a time when you felt jealous? What were you jealous about? How did it make you feel? What affects did it have on your body? How did you handle your jealousy? Could you have handled it differently? If you had, would that have made the situation better or worse?

Can you think of some things you are currently feeling jealous about? Make a list of those things. Reflect on how to turn your jealousy into something positive. For example, if you wrote down "it makes me jealous that my partner makes more money than me," reframe it in your brain and say, "I'm happy that my partner is successful." Another example is, "I'm jealous that my friend is thinner than me." Reframe it to say, "My friend motivates me to exercise more and eat healthier."

Remember, jealousy often comes from an irrational place. If it's coming from a place of hurt, consider how you can communicate this to your partner. If it's coming from a place of envy, use it to motivate yourself to work harder. Don't harbor jealousy or let it turn into resentment. Unpack the jealousy box, recycle it, and fill a new one with a healthier narrative.

■ EXERCISE ■

Consider one thing that makes you feel jealous. Now draw a picture of the green-eyed monster you face. As you draw, pay attention to your body. Do you feel yourself relaxing as you let out tension and anxiety? Are you becoming more tense as you acknowledge the jealousy you are experiencing? Who or what does the monster remind you of? Now that you are looking your own jealousy in the face, how can you overcome it? Draw another picture of yourself overcoming this green-eyed monster. You've got this!

CHEATING, AFFAIRS, AND INFIDELITY

Cheating, affairs, and infidelity are synonyms for one another to indicate a person has been unfaithful to their partner. Some research indicates that one in two couples are faced with infidelity at some point in their relationship. Other studies report that 20% of couples deal with a cheating partner. Some surveys show that it happens in 60% of relationships.

The fact of the matter is we don't know how common infidelity is. It is likely people do not feel comfortable self-reporting an affair since it is not condoned in our society. In addition, it is difficult to determine what exactly we mean when we say infidelity. It used to be cut and dried, either a one-night stand or a long-term affair. Technology and the Internet have expanded this definition for many. Nowadays, it may also include going to a strip club, sexting, or having an emotional affair with another person. I've heard people say looking at pornography, and even masturbating, are considered cheating within the confines of their relationship, often due to religious beliefs. With so many definitions, therefore, research studies are likely to continue to have inconsistent results.

Typically, it is the couple who determines what an affair is. How couples cope with infidelity is another matter. I've seen everything from people brushing it off, to blaming the partner, to blaming the person who cheated, to break-ups and divorce, to both partners taking equal responsibility for how they got to this place in their relationship. Throughout the years, I've heard people say, "If my partner ever cheated, I would leave them," but when reality hits, most people are hesitant to jump ship, particularly if children are involved or if they are financially dependent on their partner. I have also had people come into my office by themselves for therapy, confessing to infidelity and wanting to stop engaging in their hurtful behaviors, but admitting their partner doesn't have the slightest suspicion. No matter how you view things, infidelity is complicated and rarely happens in a vacuum.

Many couples also come to see me for therapy after finding out their partner had an affair. These sessions typically begin with a lot of tension and anger. The betrayed person's feelings may range from anger to sadness, while the person who had the affair may be defensive or quiet and sullen. Sessions are touch-and-go to start, but we talk about the importance of being open and honest so we can strengthen the realms of communication.

Couples are encouraged to discuss the affair so they can learn what contributing factors led up to the event. It is important for the person who was betrayed to be able to ask questions and seek clarification. However, specific details are discouraged as they end up being hurtful and provide crude visual images rather than context. This kind of detailed information almost never helps people work through the affair.

Furthermore, it's important for the person who had the affair not to be defensive. People often respond with, "I've already told you this," or "there's nothing more to tell." The betrayed person's intent is to make sure there aren't any more secret boxes. They are also in distress and might not realize they are asking the same questions repeatedly. Many people also don't like the answers they are receiving, because they don't understand the justifications being offered, so they keep asking questions hoping for a new answer. If you're the one who had an affair, try your best not to get defensive, and answer the questions being asked in an effort to repair the relationship, even if the answers don't change. The betrayed person is just trying to understand your actions. Your consistency and honesty are the start to repairing the relationship.

For both people, it is important to remember you are discussing the affair because you *want* to work through it. The affair may be brought up from time to time, even years after the initial incident. The intent of discussing the past should be just that, to have a discussion. When the past is brought up as a way to hurt someone else and is used as ammunition, the discussion becomes an argument and is just meant to be hurtful. This resolves nothing for either party.

If you decide, after working through the affair, that your partner's actions were just too hurtful and you can't get past the affair, that's okay too. You're acting after reflection, rather than reacting from a place of shock and anger.

Sex becomes complicated as people work through infidelity. The betrayed person might withhold sex due to anger and lack of trust. Withholding sex may feel like the only thing this person has control over so they deny their partner this intimate experience, as well as themselves.

As people start to work through infidelity in therapy, we talk about how to introduce sex again. The betrayed person often fears that if they "give in" and have sex with their partner, that their partner will think all is forgiven. In a therapeutic session, I help couples discuss that is not what it means at all, unless it's one of those times where it is *exactly* what it means. However, it might indicate the person is aroused and just wants to have sex. It could mean they still love you, and if you are trying to work through infidelity matters, this is probably true. It's important for the betrayed person not to withhold their own feelings and urges as a form of punishment, just as it is equally important for the person who cheated to recognize how difficult this action step may have been and that is a starting place, not an indicator of automatic resolution and forgiveness.

Case study: Jamie

Take Jamie, for example, a middle-aged man in his late forties. When he sat down in my office, I could feel the tension he was holding. After we went through his intake paperwork, I asked him to tell me a bit about himself. His shoulders relaxed as Jamie shared that he had been "happily" married to his wife Eloise for 23 years. They had two children who were in middle school. Eloise had recently gone back to work as a realtor — she had stayed home with their children while they were young. Finances were a strong suit, and Jamie elaborated he worked as a podiatrist.

When I asked what brought him to therapy, the tension in his body rose again and he stopped making eye contact with me. "I've been cheating on Elois, for years," he said, exasperated. Jamie then elaborated how he had been to various massage parlors throughout the years, building a rapport with a female masseuse, until he was able to get what he wanted, usually a "happy ending." Once he had conquered the challenge, he would find a new masseuse to pursue.

We spent a lot of time discussing his own guilt as he contemplated telling Eloise everything he had ever done. He struggled, knowing she would likely leave him if he told her the truth about years of infidelity. He also struggled with why he had had the affairs in the first place. Jamie had to open this box and slowly recognized that he enjoyed the chase, the challenge, and the thrill of something new.

Utilizing a concept from Esther Perel in her book *Mating in Captivity*, I asked Jamie, "What makes you think you have your wife?" He looked up at me, stunned, as he milled over the question. Suddenly, his attitude changed as he began to process his relationship in a whole new way, and he began to laugh until he was crying. "What makes me think I have my wife?" he said through laughter and tears, as he understood she wasn't something he owned. The point was driven home as he connected the fact that if he told her about his infidelity she *would* leave him, which is an act she would do of her own free will. This connection helped Jamie truly process his actions and invest in his marriage in ways he had never done before. He also stopped going to massage parlors after our first session.

If you've never had an affair, it might be difficult to understand why someone would betray another person in this way. Monogamy is so engrained in our society. We feel the need to honor this unspoken code when in a relationship. For many people, this isn't an issue, but for others they feel they have signed an unspoken contract without being read their rights. This can result in high conflict as couples struggle to navigate through issues of infidelity that reflect their own values.

Case study: Jules

Then there was the case of Jules, a 34-year-old successful lawyer running her own firm. From the minute she walked into my office, it was clear that Jules was intelligent, charming, and beautiful. She operated best on coffee and little sleep, and fought against herself to be a perfectionist.

Jules was in distress when she came to see me, in the perils of being in a sexual affair with a co-worker. Jules found the affair to be "energizing" but also said, "it needs to stop." Within two sessions with me, she had set a boundary with her affair partner, who was married himself, so she could focus on her own relationship. She was struggling to understand how she had gotten here, particularly as she described her husband positively. "He's a good man," she would often say in sessions.

It wasn't that she didn't believe this, it was that her statement implied she was not a good person. I encouraged her to read *When Good People Have Affairs*, by Mira Kirshenbaum. While it didn't alleviate her guilt, it did provide a platform to discuss and process her feelings and actions. It helped her identify and admit her loss of attraction to her husband, and gave her things to work on in their marriage. She was able to stop focusing on feeling like a "bad person" and instead focus on healing her relationship.

Infidelity wears many faces. It comes in many forms and affects people and relationships in a variety of ways. Sometimes people are caught cheating and have to face their partner and discuss their choices openly. Many people find this is the first time they are truly discussing the dynamics of their relationship and find they are able to have a stronger marriage after infidelity. Others find it is just too painful to work through. If you've just told your partner you've been having an affair, or you just found out your partner was cheating, allow yourself to grieve as you find a new normal. And remember, you don't want to go back to the "way things were" because something wasn't working. The goal is to move forward, creating an honest and trustworthy bond, whether that's together or with someone else.

▪ EXERCISE ▪

Part of working through infidelity is taking responsibility for how you contributed to it. It also requires listening and validating your partner. This can be particularly difficult for the person who was betrayed. Additionally, you have to navigate some really icky feelings as you work to reestablish the trust that was lost.

- Were you the one who cheated?
- How did you contribute to the affair?
- Did you ignore your partner's needs?
- Were you fighting frequently?
- Are you mad at yourself? Your partner?
- Do you want to work through the aftermath of the affair to save the relationship? If yes, why is it worth it? If no, why can't you?
- What is one tangible thing your partner can do this week to help meet your needs and start to reestablish trust?

If you feel comfortable, discuss the answers with your partner over a Pancake Talk, illustrated in the *Fantasy* chapter. If you aren't ready to discuss this difficult topic, take time for yourself to answer and process these questions alone. Consider talking through them with a therapist who can help you navigate your feelings.

SEX ADDICTION

Have you heard the term sex addiction? It has been made a very popular phrase by the media, by those affected by infidelity, and marketing rehab programs. What do people mean when they talk about sex addiction? What is a sex addict? Is it someone who looks at pornography a few times a week? Someone who looks at pornography every day? Is it someone who stars in pornography movies? Someone who masturbates daily? A person who fantasizes about someone other than their partner? Someone who is having an affair? Is a sex addict someone who engages in risky sexual behavior? Never uses a condom? Has multiple partners? Doesn't reveal their STI or STD status to a sexual partner? Someone who pays a prostitute for sex? Solicits people on the Internet for sex? Has a kink or fetish they engage in?

With groups like Sex Addicts Anonymous and Sexaholics Anonymous, celebrities such as Tiger Woods and Charlie Sheen, and treatment centers across the United States, the words "sex addiction" are buzz words that have gotten a lot of hype. However, it can be difficult to decipher what sex addiction actually is.

It may all seem like semantics as the phrasing has created heated debates among mental health professionals. Because there is so much debate about what qualifies as a sex addict, the definition varies drastically. Even if someone does personally identify with the label itself, it should be noted it is not diagnosable by a professional. Sex addiction is not in the Diagnostic and Statistical Manual, which means there are no criteria for making a diagnosis, and therefore it is not considered a mental health disorder. So, while sex addiction is a subject of debate, neither AASECT nor many other professional organizations consider risky or compulsive sexual behavior an addiction.

If you're like many folks, you might do research about sex addiction to help understand your problematic sexual choices or your partner's. You'll likely find several quizzes online you can take, and with the click of a few buttons you may be told to seek treatment. The Sex Addiction Screening Test (SAST) is one of the most well known, a quiz which utilizes 52 questions to assess the kind of help you need, although there appear to be many versions of this test on various websites. The SAST was "designed to assist in the assessment of sexually compulsive behavior which may indicate the presence of sex addiction" (recoveryzone.com). Questions include asking if you engage in kink and fetishes, partake in online dating, and those who have experienced post-coital tristesse (or the post-sex blues).

While taking the SAST, or another online quiz, is free, people who are told they are addicted to sex are then encouraged to seek out a treatment program. Some of these programs cost thousands of dollars, time away from home and work, and intensive therapy. Since this is not a realistic option for many people, a person may decide to attend a support group like Sex Addicts Anonymous, which they can attend for free. Sex Addicts Anonymous discusses that recovery is possible when people have "accepted the fact that we were powerless over our addictive sexual behavior," following the 12-step model. This language not only removes all responsibility from the person for their choices and actions, but also leaves loved ones feeling hopefulness because they just have to accept their partner has no control over their actions. In reality, this just isn't true.

Sexual behavior can be problematic. Helping someone whose sexual behavior is out of control is a big box that should be carefully sorted through, but not from a shame-based perspective. The issue is almost never the sex that a person is having, but the risk or deception involved. There are many people dealing with anxiety, trauma, anger, or resentment and they choose to deal with those issues by engaging in problematic sexual behavior. The goal in treating out of control sexual behavior is not to shame the person for utilizing sex as their outlet to cope with their trauma, but to address the box of trauma so they can stop utilizing sex as their outlet. So let's shed the label that enables and get to the crux of the issue.

Case study: Andrew

Andrew scheduled a session shortly after a website known for helping men discreetly have affairs was hacked into. He was a dentist in his early 50s and had been married to his wife for 17 years. They had two high-school age children. Andrew said he had cheated on his wife dozens of times and recounted his infidelity during therapy. He shared how he utilized opportunities to have affairs at professional conferences, would get massages in parlors where he knew he could turn the experience into a "happy ending," and had set up multiple fake online accounts so he could prowl dating websites. He boasted that his wife had never caught him.

I questioned why he chose to engage in these behaviors and I asked about his sex life with his wife. Initially, he wasn't sure why he behaved the way he did, but he recognized he didn't like who he had become. He said he loved having sex with his wife most. He expressed wishing they had more frequent sex, which had waned over the years due to having kids and his wife starting her own business.

Admittedly, he had never had a conversation with his wife about their sex life. Rather than address it with her, he chose to engage in problematic sexual behavior. He knew it had been a problem for many years, but the thought of his wife finding out about his infidelity after the website he had been on was hacked encouraged him to reach out for help.

Andrew's situation may be relatable for many. He had poor communication skills and even worse coping skills. To learn more about why he engaged in high-risk sexual behaviors and was making poor choices, we discussed his relationship with his wife in-depth and also talked about his upbringing. He had grown up in an upper-middle class home. His father was a doctor while his mother stayed at home to care for his younger brother, who had cerebral palsy. There was a lot of pressure on Andrew to be successful, and his parent's way of encouraging him and showing love was to reward him for good grades and sports accomplishments.

The environment set him up to expect instant gratification. Winning was equated to success. Andrew was able to identify the unspoken messages he received growing up and stored in a box, and he felt he was taught that if someone couldn't offer you something, then they were not worth your time.

He admitted that he would sneak into his brother's room at night, hold him and cry sometimes. I asked why he did this, and with tears in his eyes he said he loved his brother so much, and was angry at his parents for thinking his brother couldn't have success, and for putting all of the burden on him. Andrew noted that he was starved for affection growing up. It was all about success, and suddenly he realized his brother was the only one who received touch because his parents had to physically assist him everyday. He would sneak into his brother's bed to have that physical affection, but said it was also his way of taking some of his parents' affection, by "stealing" it from his brother.

As he grew older, Andrew continued to thrive from instant gratification and winning, but also wanted the physical touch and intimacy that was missing from his life, so he began to womanize. When he met his wife at age 34, he fell in love. He had never been in love and he thought she could change his ways. He said he was faithful the first three years of their marriage, until he had his first affair at a conference. Recalling the thrill of the chase, and knowing he wasn't going to get caught, his old patterns picked back up. Andrew realized he was engaging in some risky behaviors and was putting his wife at risk by having intercourse with other people.

It took several months of therapy, but once Andrew was able to identify why he was engaging in problematic sexual behavior, he was able to finally start working through his feelings towards his parents and his upbringing. Andrew continued individual therapy with me while he and his wife went to couples therapy to work on improving their communication skills. He wanted to focus on improving their relationship and he made a conscious choice to invest in his marriage and create a new box with his wife.

The story of Andrew shows us that there is a something more going on than cheating behaviors. It is a story about a man with trauma in his childhood who was not given the physical affection a child needs, and who never learned to cope with rejection, disappointment, or failure. Andrew was able to recognize that his sexual behavior was problematic, and he felt a lot of guilt and shame when he began therapy. He felt like he was out of control, addicted to sex, and unsure how to address it. Andrew wanted to take accountability for his actions and knew that ultimately he did have control over his actions. He just needed help sorting through all of his boxes, understanding why he was making the choices he had been making, and learning to cope.

Case study: Brian

In the world of sex addiction, the term pornography addict has also made a name for itself. It is, once again, difficult to define what a pornography addict actually is. I've had men—it is almost always men—say they were addicted to pornography because they watch it twice a week or because they aren't watching it with their wife. On the other extreme, I've had men like Brian, who said he was watching pornography six hours a night, in the bathroom at work, and would cancel plans with friends because he wanted to watch pornography instead. Brian was engaging in problematic sexual behavior and it was affecting his personal life and putting his professional career at risk.

Through therapy, Brian identified he was utilizing pornography to deal with extreme anxiety. It was a box he continued to fill, but never unpacked. More specifically, he was utilizing pornography so he would not have to unpack his box of anxiety. Pornography was his way of coping. While the use of pornography did curb his feelings of anxiety initially, it had become so habitual that he didn't know how to incorporate other coping skills. He was reliant on the use of pornography to ease his anxiety. It had come to a point that he was not dealing with his anxiety anymore. He was avoiding it by looking at pornography.

To start working through this anxiety and developing healthy coping skills, Brian agreed to take some immediate steps to change his behavior. For starters, he put a "pornography block" on his phone so he would not have access readily available, specifically at work. At home, he moved his desk out of his bedroom and put it near a window in the living room so he would have to consider who might see him if he looked at pornography. He also began to track his anxiety so he could identify when, and why, he was having anxiety, in an effort to address it in a healthier manner. These immediate changes, in addition to therapy and engaging in lots of self-introspection, began to alter the way Brian utilized pornography and how he felt about it. He realized there was nothing morally or ethically wrong with looking at pornography for him, but he was utilizing it for all the wrong reasons.

At the end of the day, whether you identify with the label sex addict or not, you *can* make different choices. You can work through your past or trauma to understand your choices. You can acknowledge how your choices affect others. You can let go of the guilt and shame you carry. You can have a healthy sexual relationship with yourself. You can have a healthy sexual relationship with a partner.

■ EXERCISE ■

Is your sexual behavior problematic? These three questions are pertinent to answering that question.

1. Are you hurting yourself?
2. Are you hurting anyone else?
3. Is it illegal?

If you answer yes to any of these questions, you should seek out an AASECT Certified Sex Therapist to help you sort through this, particularly if the behavior is illegal.

Once you've answered these initial questions, you can begin to reflect deeper to determine why your sexual behavior is problematic for you. Are you missing out on time with friends or family to engage in the behavior? Is your job at risk? Are you in debt? Are you avoiding dealing with trauma, anxiety, or conflict? Be accountable for your actions and begin to reflect on why you are making the choices you are making.

If you need to make immediate changes, here are some simple action steps you can take:

- Put a pornography block on your phone or computer.
- Put your computer in the living room so it's not located in a private area.
- Avoid strip clubs and bars.
- Ask a friend to be your accountability buddy and check in on you or spend time with you.
- Make plans with friends, family, or co-workers so you have obligations to meet.
- Commit to a project at work.
- Take on a part-time job.
- Find an AASECT Certified Sex Therapist to talk to.
- Find other healthy distractions while you find out why you are utilizing sex in an unhealthy manner.

■ EXERCISE ■

In order to change our behaviors, we have to open a few boxes and recognize how we filled them in the first place. We often make snap decisions, before we even think about if it is good for us or how it will make us feel. Oftentimes, this isn't an issue, as it creates habits. However, consider a time you've mindlessly walked to the fridge, opened it up, stared at the contents for a minute, and shut it without grabbing anything to eat. You may even wander back and open it up again a few minutes later. Why did you do this? Were you even hungry? Being aware of *why* we make decisions can help us make different ones, or at least confirm the choices we are already making. When we engage in things mindlessly it can be difficult to break the routine. The habit becomes a vicious cycle. We may know we want to make a different choice, but we don't know *how*.

This exercise is to help you recognize why you are making the choices you make, but also helps you find a way to off-ramp, thus making a different choice. It was created for Aurora Mental Health in Aurora, CO by therapists John J. Murphy, LCSW, and David J. Berry, LCSW. Below the questions you will see a silly example about eating cupcakes, which you can then apply to your own problematic behavior:

1. What is your emotional state? How are you **feeling**? This is where the cycle starts so it's really important to identify this.

2. What's **triggering** you to engage in the behavior? A trigger is ignited by one of your five senses (sight, hearing, taste, smell, or touch).

3. What are you thinking now that you've been triggered? What are your immediate **thoughts**?

4. Are you experiencing any **body changes**? What are they? How are you feeling?

5. What is your **fantasy**? What do you hope will happen?

6. What do you tell yourself to **justify** your actions so you don't feel guilty? [INSERT ACTION] You are now engaging in the behavior.

7. Now that you've engaged in the action, do you feel guilty? What are you **feeling guilty** about?

8. How do you justify your actions to alleviate your guilt? What do you tell yourself to make yourself **feel better**?

9. We continue to engage in the same cycles because ultimately they create a positive memory. What is the **positive memory** you have?

Example:

1. I'm feeling bored, lonely, and hungry.

2. I see an advertisement on television for baking cupcakes.

3. I wish I had a cupcake right now. I'm so hungry. If I could just have one cupcake I would be satisfied.

4. My stomach growls. I feel excited.

5. I will make red velvet cupcakes and eat them all. I will be full and happy.

6. I tell myself that the calories do not matter.

7. I shouldn't have eaten all those cupcakes.

8. No one will know I ate all those cupcakes. Plus, I will exercise tomorrow.

9. Those cupcakes tasted delicious.

Using the example above, you should write a cycle about the problematic sexual behavior you are engaging in. If you are engaging in multiple behaviors, you may need to create multiple cycles, as the motivation to engage in each one may look different. As you begin to understand why you are engaging in the behaviors you write about, you can start to recognize what is happening to your body, your thoughts and feelings, and make a choice to off-ramp before the fantasy occurs. Once you are past the fantasy, you've engaged in the behavior.

One of my clients in therapy would create a cycle *every single time* he looked at pornography, and he made the cycle a consequence for engaging in a behavior he didn't really want to be doing. What would motivate you to make changes and off-ramp from your cycle?

SEXUAL ABUSE CYCLE

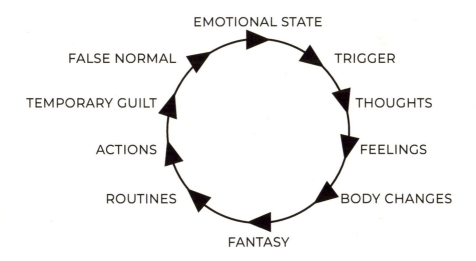

PORNOGRAPHY

Everyone has a box with feelings about pornography. Some people think it is great to view erotic images with the quick click of a button. Others think it is morally wrong, believe it is tearing relationships apart, and would vote to have it legally banned. Most people aren't neutral about pornography and tend to have an opinion of some sort that lies somewhere in the middle.

Unfortunately, this bias is also reflected when attempting to do research about pornography. There are a lot of statistics about pornography and its effects on people, but these statistics often lack citations, research, or evidence. Many are supported by bias, based on if the researcher is for or against pornography. I always say you'll also get what you search for. If you search for information supporting evidence of pornography addiction, that is exactly what you will find. If you search for information about the myth of sex addiction, then that is what you will find. At the end of the day, feelings about pornography are most often based on values.

There are thousands upon thousands of pornography websites, with millions of visitors to these sites each month. It is difficult to estimate just how many websites cater to pornography. At best, data is inconsistent. Some statistics indicate that half of all websites on the Internet are pornography-based, while others say it's a mere 4%. The truth probably lies somewhere in there but it is unlikely we'll ever have an exact number, due to the daily fluctuation of websites and their domains.

One pornography website containing adult content, Pornhub, has been collecting data and insights from their users since 2013. The data collected is considered internal research by a team of statisticians who work at Pornhub. What's collected is still considered raw data, as there is no statistical analysis on this information. The site describes itself as "the #1 free pornography site in the world with hundreds of thousands of free videos, including free HD and downloading capabilities." At the time of print, they reported having 100 million visitors *per day*. With so many visitors, it is beneficial for statisticians to track user data and viewer trends.

Reviewing Pornhub's searches for specific content on their website helps shed light on current pornography trends. In the United States, the most searched for term is "lesbian," a trend that has been consistent for years. However, current trends and social media influences also tend to affect pornography searches. Trends tend to be popular for about 12–18 months on average because consumers get bored quickly. So while they are unlikely to remain trends, it is interesting to note what Pornhub's insight team has found to be popular trends over the years, including fidget spinners and the popular video game Fortnite.

The results from Pornhub's extensive data collection have also revealed when people view pornography the most. Consistent for the last few years, most people are viewing pornography between 10 PM and midnight, with Sunday being the most popular day for viewers to engage. While Pornhub has users from all over the world, most users are from the United States. Men tend to look at pornography more frequently than women, but about a quarter of Pornhub's visitors do identify as women.

Now we know when people view pornography, but where do they do it? With the use of cell phones and improved technology, most people viewing pornography tend to do it from their phone. However, viewing declines during live sporting events, such as the Super Bowl. If you are interested in more facts and research, you can visit Pornhub's insights on their website, which are updated annually.

While Pornhub's data and insights are useful and fascinating, further research is needed to evaluate trends in pornography. At times, data is collected from surveys and studies at universities, colleges, and online. Self-reporting and unreliable sample sizes make the data inconsistent, though. It is difficult to obtain funding for research related to sexuality, due to ethical limitations and social stigma. Although more reliable research is needed, data is beginning to offer some additional understanding. For example, research shows that on average boys look at pornography for the first time at age ten. Unfortunately, research on exposure for girls is less available. Typically, exposure is usually "accidental" the first time, rather than being intentionally sought out.

Exposure to pornography has also changed over time with the availability of the Internet and cellular phones. My clients over age 40 recall finding their father's *Playboy* and *Hustler* magazines under their parent's bed or in a box in the garage. Younger clients remember dial-up Internet, which became popular in the late 90s. At that time, pop-up ads were ubiquitous. Ads for pornography were common, and directed the user to their website. Nowadays, it's easy to access pornography.

Personal beliefs and values have the biggest influence over how we feel about pornography. If you're single, your beliefs and values about pornography probably aren't affecting anyone else.

Typically the box we fill with beliefs and values about pornography, among other things we value, are opened when we are in relationship. It is at these times our beliefs and values impact others and help us determine if we want to be in a relationship with someone. Common values stem from our religious beliefs, whether to have kids, and how we view finances. Many couples do not talk about their values relating to pornography until it becomes an issue for one partner in the relationship.

Case study: Tyler and Blair

This was the case for Tyler and Blair. The couple, together for four years, engaged for five months, had been having a casual conversation with friends on a double date. The conversation had quickly turned from cherry pie to whipped cream to sex. The other couple they were with had a few drinks and had begun to over-share. They mentioned looking at pornography together and even making their own sex videos. Blair became squirmy and uncomfortable as the couple pressed Tyler and Blair about their sex life. "You don't look at pornography, do you?" she asked Tyler. Tyler began to laugh nervously while the other couple burst into chuckles. "Of course he looks at porn!" the other woman said.

When they got home that evening, Blair went straight to bed. She was not sure how to process this information, but could feel herself getting upset. The next day Blair confronted Tyler. "I can't believe you've been hiding this from me," she accused him. The conversation quickly derailed as he became defensive, and she began to criticize. When the couple came to see me for therapy a few months later, things had not improved.

Blair said she felt like Tyler was cheating on her every time he looked at pornography. She even thought perhaps he was a sex addict. She had begun to check his phone and monitor his laptop history. Tyler said he felt violated and betrayed because Blair was "snooping" on him. He said he only looked at pornography when he masturbated, which was five to seven times per week. "That's too much!" Blair exclaimed.

After both of them opened their own box to share their viewpoints, it was obvious why they had made no movement on the subject. They were both flooded with emotion and had no capacity to hear what the other person was saying. Tyler felt like Blair was blowing the whole thing out of proportion and was resentful the issue had led them to therapy, while Blair felt he was cheating on her and not attracted to her anymore.

We spent some time discussing each of their upbringings to help determine how their backgrounds influenced their values on pornography. By exploring their respective upbringings, they were able to have a dialogue about the messages they received growing up about sexuality. Tyler admitted he had never really thought about how his upbringing influenced his ideas of sexuality, but said viewing pornography had been a part of his masturbation routine since he was 14. He said his parents never talked to him about pornography usage, but his peers normalized it. In addition, Tyler did not feel it impacted his sexual attraction to Blair, and so he struggled to understand what the issue was.

Blair had grown up in a household where she received a lot of mixed messages. Raised by a single mother who identified as a feminist, Blair was told pornography was bad and contributed to the objectification of women. However, while Blair's mother made it clear that she believed objectifying women was not part of a healthy sexual repertoire, she did not share what was healthy, nor did she talk about any aspect of pornography that could be healthy. Blair very much believed that viewing pornography was going to cause irreparable damage to her relationship with Tyler because of these influences. "If this isn't resolved, I don't think I can stay in the relationship," she admitted. This was devastating to Tyler, but also gave the couple grounds to have a conversation about their drastically differing perspectives.

To help facilitate the discussion and truly examine the contents in each of their boxes, I asked the couple to do the exercise at the end of this chapter to help determine their own values. Each of them was encouraged to process how they felt and discuss how their upbringing influenced their beliefs and values about pornography.

The goal of this exercise was not to change anyone's point of view, but to help the other person understand where they were coming from and take ownership of their beliefs. I asked them to fill it out at home and, once they completed it, we discussed it in their next session.

After taking some time in sessions to improve communication, Blair was able to take ownership for her own body image issues and acknowledge how they were impacting her views of pornography. "I just know I'll never look like any of those women," she expressed. "My boobs will never be that perky, my hair will never be that blond, and I definitely will never be able to spread my legs that far apart."

Tyler offered reassurance that he was not interested in being intimate with the women in the videos. "Whenever I watch porn, I imagine those women are you," he confided. Blair was shocked and slightly less hurt. She was also able to admit that her trust issues stemmed from her previous relationship with a man who had cheated on her. She felt like pornography was Tyler's way of beginning to stray and look at other women. After he explained how he views pornography, she felt less threatened by the women in the videos.

I also asked Tyler to take responsibility for his contributions to the couple's conflict. He admitted he should have talked to Blair early on in the relationship about pornography. "I guess I thought it was my thing, so I never thought this would affect her." While he felt his masturbation habits were private, he understood why Blair's past made it feel like his pornography habits were being kept a secret.

Tyler also realized there were times he did choose to look at pornography and masturbate instead of initiating sex with Blair. While this was hurtful to Blair, admitting it out loud gave Tyler the opportunity to process it and think about why he was making this choice. This behavior had increased more over the last few months because they had been fighting. While discussing his actions, I was able to help him recognize that he believed he was doing Blair a favor.

"I just like having sex more than her and I didn't want to make her feel obligated to have sex with me if she was not in the mood to." As I helped him process this, Blair pointed out that he was making a choice for her, so she did not even get to make a decision. By the end of their time in therapy, they were able to repack their boxes so they could understand and validate one another and negotiate what felt comfortable for them both.

No matter where you stand on the issue, everyone has feelings about pornography. It is important to understand your own beliefs and values. It is equally important to know where your partner stands and why. The following exercise will help you evaluate your feelings on the issue.

▪ EXERCISE ▪

It is important to consider your own feelings about pornography to determine what morals and values your feelings are based on. The following chart will help you assess how you feel about pornography. Have your partner complete the exercise too, so you can have the discussion to follow.

I Think Porn is...

For each question, circle **Yes** if you agree with the statement, **No** if you don't. You will not be asked to share your responses.

Yes / No Actors in pornographic films should be required to use barrier methods that protect against HIV and other sexually-transmitted infections (STIs).

Yes / No If someone looks at pornography, it means they are not sexually aroused by their current partner.

Yes / No If someone watches pornography, it's best if they keep it private.

Yes / No Individuals who view too much porn will not have a healthy sexual relationship with another person.

Yes / No It's okay for an individual to want to perform in a pornographic scene.

Yes / No Once a couple decides to be monogamous, neither person should seek out sexually explicit material.

Yes / No People need to just accept that porn is a part of life, and not worry about who is watching whom do what.

Yes / No Pornography is degrading to women.

Yes / No The government should place more regulations on the porn industry.

Yes / No The sex shown in porn should always be clearly consensual and demonstrate the use of external or internal barrier methods such as condoms.

Yes / No There should be age restrictions placed on who can purchase sexually explicit material.

Yes / No Viewing pornography can be a healthy sexual experience when by yourself.

Yes / No Watching porn in secret will damage a relationship.

What Pornography Includes, What it Leaves Out

For each statement below, circle **Yes** if it can be learned from pornography, **No** if not, and **Maybe** if you have mixed reactions.

Yes / Maybe / No Possible ways of achieving sexual pleasure.

Yes / Maybe / No How to talk about sex with a partner.

Yes / Maybe / No Various types of sexual behavior.

Yes / Maybe / No Common ways that most adults have sex.

Yes / Maybe / No Types of images that might be shocking.

Yes / Maybe / No How to say "no" to unwanted sexual behavior.

Yes / Maybe / No Standards for how to treat a partner in a relationship.

Yes / Maybe / No Images that might enable arousal and orgasm.

Yes / Maybe / No How normal bodies generally look.

Yes / Maybe / No Common ways that people have sex.

Yes / Maybe / No What a partner will be willing to try.

Yes / Maybe / No Safer-sex practices for preventing pregnancy and sexually transmitted infections (STIs).

Yes / Maybe / No Sex involving an emotional connection to another person.

Yes / Maybe / No What a real-life partner would find pleasing.

Yes / Maybe / No The emotional effects of sexual violence.

Yes / Maybe / No Signs that the men portrayed in pornography are sexually aroused.

Yes / Maybe / No How to be a good sexual partner.

Yes / Maybe / No A method for distinguishing fantasy from reality.

Yes / Maybe / No A guide for how you would like sex to be in real life.

Yes / Maybe / No Signs that the women portrayed in pornography are sexually aroused.

KINK

Let's start with a few definitions before we get kinky. *Kink* is an umbrella term—it refers to an unconventional sexual preference or behavior. A *fetish* is when a person has a sexual desire for an object, body part, or specific activity. In contrast, *paraphilia,* a term utilized by the Diagnostic and Statistical Manual, is "any intense and persistent sexual interest other than sexual interest in genital stimulation" with "consenting human partners" (DSM, 2013, p. 685). Both fetishes and paraphilias are kinks. Some people act on their kinks while others maintain them only as sexual fantasies. Joyal (p. 328) says,

> *From a clinical point of view, determining when a sexual fantasy, usual or not, is a disorder is fairly straightforward: it is obligatory, compulsive, and/ or results in sexual dysfunction or causes distress or impairment to the individual.*

Sexual fetishes and paraphilias are most common among heterosexual men. Rates of occurrence are difficult to determine, as someone who is distressed might seek therapy, but someone who has accepted the fetish would not. Stigmas attached to fetishes also prevent people from seeking therapy. For example, someone who is attracted to children, but has not acted on it, might be too ashamed to seek therapy for fear of judgment. The distressing thoughts may be too unbearable to handle alone, though, and a trusted therapist can help someone stay in control of these thoughts. Since the trouble this kind of paraphilia causes also borders on legalities and cannot safely be acted out, seeking out a trusted therapist is imperative.

Case study: Terrell

Typically the onset of a kink or fetish occurs at puberty. No one is really sure why. Clients who come in with a sexual fetish tend to have a very distinct memory of when they developed the fetish. Terrell vividly recalled playing dress-up with his older sister when he was six. They were putting on princess dresses and their mother's high heels. "I've never wanted to be a girl," he insisted, "but I remember the feeling of putting on my mother's pantyhose. It was before I associated feelings of shame with it. They were so silky and smooth."

I could see him grasping onto the memory of a six-year-old boy who felt safe and confident. While plenty of other young boys have played dress-up with their sisters, Terrell's experience turned into a pantyhose fetish. As he grew up, and it was made clear by others that his interest was not socially acceptable, he would steal his mother's and sister's garments to masturbate to. It's unclear why Terrell's experience turned into a fetish, while someone else just has a distant memory of playing dress-up with his sister. Regardless, the memory for many people is very clear and distinct, as if it happened yesterday.

When people come to therapy to discuss their kink, it's typically for one of three reasons: they want to eradicate their kink, they are unsure how to tell a partner about their kink, or their partner doesn't accept their kink. Disclaimer: I *cannot* eradicate a fetish. Even if I could, I wouldn't. Anyone who says they can, can't. If you want to abstain from your fetish, read the chapter on *Sex Addiction* and complete the exercise at the end of the chapter. When someone has this goal in mind it is because the kink causes them distress and they feel shame, embarrassment, and guilt. I am very transparent that I cannot eradicate a kink, but I am also very empathetic to the distress it causes. I've met men who have had a kink for 40 years, and have never told another soul about it.

For some people, a kink is like a shadow following them, mocking them for being different. Debbie Ford, author and creator of The Ford Institute, elaborates on her website:

> *Our shadow is made up of all the parts of ourselves that we hide, deny, suppress, and don't see in ourselves — both the positive and the negative. Our shadow is all the aspects that we reject out of shame, fear, or disapproval. It is made up of any part of ourselves that we believe is unacceptable, will be met with disapproval by others, or that annoys, horrifies or disgusts us about other people or about ourselves.*

Your shadow, and your kink, is part of you.

When trying to unpack the box of feelings filled with guilt, shame, and embarrassment caused by a kink, I always ask, "Are you hurting yourself? Are you hurting someone else?" Almost always, the person is not. Not physically, anyway. So, in therapy, I will help the client process their feelings of shame around the fetish. Clients process these feelings as they start to unpack the box of guilt. As they begin to fill a new box with feelings of self-trust, feelings of worthlessness diminish. Over time, people start to find a place of acceptance and self-love and accept their shadow.

Case study: Dylan

Dylan was a handsome and charismatic man who came to see me for therapy. Beneath his charisma and charm, though, Dylan was insecure and anxious. Initially, I had to prod to get him to open up about basic demographic information, but when I asked him what brought him in to therapy, he jumped in like a fish in water. He told me he had been struggling with a foot fetish for as long as he could remember, before it became sexual in nature. Bare feet were his weakness and he both longed for, and loathed, long summer nights. He enjoyed being able to see bare feet all around him, but summertime was also a constant reminder of the shame and guilt he felt.

While he discussed his fetish, his shame seemed to fade, almost as if it were someone else telling his story. He only stopped short when he got to the heart of the problem: Samantha. Dylan had been dating Samantha, a female entrepreneur, for the last eight months. "I want to ask her to marry me, but I'm worried if she knows about my fetish, she'll say no. I'm worried I need it too. I'm scared to be alone," he finished, not really referring to his relationship with Samantha anymore.

"I sense you already feel that way," I stated.

After two months in therapy, Dylan had worked through his own guilt. In fact, he didn't seem to feel guilty about his fetish at all unless we were talking about Samantha. When discussing his relationship, he became a different person as his confidence faded away. Working through *why* he was feeling guilty provided him the initiative he needed to confide in Samantha that he had been going to therapy, and he asked her to attend a session with him.

Samantha was clearly nervous under the circumstances, but relaxed as I offered her some humor. It took Dylan half the session and a lot of small talk to finally say, "I have something to tell you." Samantha's small stature looked defeated as she awaited his confession. Dylan looked down at the floor, and said quietly, "I have a foot fetish. My whole life. I love you. I've worked really hard to make it go away. I've worked harder to accept who I am." A look of relief overcame Samantha as she let out a deep sigh and began to laugh and cry at the same time.

Unsure what to think, Dylan looked to me for advice. "How are you feeling right now?" I asked her, the stereotypical therapy question.

She took a tissue and dabbed at her eyes. "I couldn't fathom why you were taking me to see a *sex therapist!* I thought you were cheating on me," she exclaimed, and then she began to laugh. While Samantha did admit she had some adjusting to do, she attended a few sessions with Dylan to work through her initial shock, find her own level of acceptance, and find a compromise with Dylan. This story had a happy ending and the couple became engaged three months later.

Another reason people come to see me is because one person has a kink, and the other person does *not* accept it. They may say they don't want anything to do with it, try to forbid the person from acting on it, and even say they are disgusted by it. It puts both people in a difficult position and neither feels good about the conflict.

Case study: Charlie

Charlie, a man in his early 30s, had been married to his wife Courtney for two years. They had a one-year-old daughter and, to an outsider, their life seemed good. Charlie was a manager for a local construction company and his wife stayed home with their baby. The first session, Charlie came alone so he could share where he was at without judgment, although he looked down at the floor when he talked, as if he was judging himself.

Ever since Charlie was a boy, he'd had an "obsession" of sorts with gloves, and as he got older they began to carry sexual appeal. "I just love the texture on me, while, um, being intimate," he confided. "I told Courtney way before we got married. This is just a part of who I am and I wanted to be up front about that. I want her to wear gloves on occasion while we're having sexy time." In the last few years, he said he had purchased a few pairs for Courtney to wear, but they all ended up in a drawer. Whenever he would bring up the subject, she would just scowl at him.

Courtney came to the next therapy session. She sat with her arms crossed and had the same scowl on her face. "Yeah, he told me about it before we got married. I thought it was weird but, whatever. We have a daughter now. I don't want her being subjected to something so deviant."

Charlie shot back at her, "Gloves are deviant?" Charlie and Courtney were in a place of conflict and they weren't listening to one another. They both felt they were right, and had hit a roadblock. If this feels similar to the conflict in your relationship, start with the *Communication* chapter before continuing.

It took several sessions to improve this couple's communication, but once we did, we were able to discuss the issue directly. Courtney was able to address why she felt uncomfortable with Charlie's glove fetish in a way that was non-judgmental. "It just feels like Charlie could be having sex with anyone wearing gloves and that makes sex feel impersonal. It's hurtful. It feels like the object of his desire is the gloves, not me," she shared in therapy.

Charlie was also able to explain his frustrations. "I feel like I have been open and honest about this fetish from the beginning."

While gloves were not sexual for Courtney at all, she was able to work through her feelings and display empathy for Charlie. This couple worked hard to provide validation and reassurance to one another. Courtney's demeanor softened the more sessions we had and she was able to view Charlie as her spouse and the gloves as an object, not her enemy.

If you are struggling with a sexual fetish, or with a partner's fetish, you are not alone. People are unsure how to process kinks or fetishes due to negative associations. With some patience, processing, and understanding, we can find a way forward to accept others for their quirks and unique qualities.

■ EXERCISE ■

If you read this chapter because you are struggling to accept your kink and yourself, this exercise is for you. First consider: are you hurting yourself? Are you hurting someone else? As previously mentioned, you cannot eradicate a fetish, but if it is causing you harm or distress, please refer to the chapter on *Sex Addiction* and create a cycle to help yourself feel in control of the fetish, instead of it having control over you. If instead you are struggling to open this box and accept that you're just a bit different, then this exercise is for you.

Start by getting a notebook and finding a quiet place to write. Make yourself comfortable and surround yourself with things that feel validating. In the notebook, make a list of all the reasons you have sex. Be sure to include the kink or fetish as one of the reasons if it is sexually arousing for you. It is presumable that you have listed several other things. The fetish is *only* one of them.

Now make another list. This list should be all of the things that make you unique. Once again, be sure to include the fetish. Once you've written the entire list, look at it. Notice the fetish doesn't make you who you are. There are *so* many things that make you who you are.

Okay, one more list! We all have things we dislike about ourselves, but remember what Carl Jung said: *"There is no light without shadow and no psychic wholeness without imperfection."*

Make a list of your imperfections and the negative judgments you have about yourself. The idea of Debbie Ford's shadow work is that the qualities we loathe about others, we have ourselves. These are the parts of yourself you may dislike and try to hide, such as your kink. You may find yourself thinking thoughts like, "I wouldn't want to be with someone like me," and then you find yourself feeling guilty, ashamed, and trying to hide your kink.

Go through your entire list and change each thought on the list to something positive. Your own uniqueness is not something to be ashamed of. For every imperfection and negative judgment you have about yourself, consider how it also serves a purpose. For example, you may think, "No one will love me like this. I'm just too weird." However, I bet this view of yourself has made you more accepting of others who don't quite fit in. The new sentence may read, "My lack of acceptance for myself has turned into acceptance for others."

■ EXERCISE ■

If you are unsure how to tell a partner about your kink, this exercise is for you. First, review the Pancake Talk exercise from the *Fantasy* chapter. This is essential to setting up an environment that is supportive for you both. Next, be honest with yourself and determine *what* you need to share with your partner, and consider *why* you are sharing it. Prioritize those needs for the initial conversation so you do not overwhelm your partner with information. Keep it short and sweet. "Honey, I need to tell you something. It's taken me a long time to accept who I am and it is difficult to share it with you now. I am sharing this because I think it's important to be honest with you and I don't believe you will judge me. I have a kink." Reassure your partner that the kink doesn't change who you are and that you do not expect them to process this information immediately. Give them space so they don't feel compelled to respond right away, give time for them to process, and allow them to ask questions.

▪ EXERCISE ▪

If your partner is struggling to accept your kink, this exercise is for you. Below is a checklist of sexual and intimate activities. Go through the checklist and decide what things are always okay, sometimes okay, or never okay. Complete the list individually and then discuss as a couple. The intention is to show we all have different sexual preferences, which can vary each day based on our energy and mood. The list shows there are many sexual and intimate activities to choose, including your kink (which you can list in the Other category). See what aligns for you both, and what differs. Discuss your likenesses and differences. Find compromise within them.

____ Holding hands

____ Hugging

____ Pecking on the lips

____ Kissing on the cheek

____ Being kissed on the cheek

____ Being kissed on the neck

____ Kissing someone on the neck

____ Having your ear bitten/nibbled

____ Biting/nibbling someone's ear

____ Stimulating/kissing someone's nipples/breasts

____ Having your nipples/breasts stimulated and kissed

____ Giving a back massage

____ Receiving a back massage

____ Taking a shower with someone

____ Having your fingers/toes sucked on orally

___ Sucking on someone else's fingers/toes with your mouth

___ Inserting your fingers into someone's vagina

___ Having fingers inserted inside your vagina

___ Touching/rubbing someone's penis with your hand

___ Having your penis touched/rubbed by a hand

___ Masturbating in front of someone

___ Watching someone else masturbate in front of you

___ Mutual masturbation

___ Grinding (dry humping)

___ Having the outside of your anus stimulated by hand

___ Stimulating the outside of someone's anus with your hand

___ Giving oral sex

___ Receiving oral sex

___ Having your anus licked

___ Licking someone's anus

___ Having something inserted into your anus (fingers, toy, etc.)

___ Inserting something into someone's anus (fingers, toy, etc.)

___ Receiving anal intercourse

___ Giving anal intercourse

___ Having penile-vaginal intercourse

___ Having a sex toy used on you

___ Using a sex toy on someone

___ Having lubricant rubbed on your nipples/breasts

___ Rubbing lubricant on someone's nipples/breasts

___ Having lubricant rubbed on your genitals

___ Rubbing lubricant on someone's genitals

___ Ejaculating onto someone's body/mouth

___ Being ejaculated onto your body/mouth

___ Being bitten/scratched/slapped

___ Biting/scratching/slapping someone else

___ Wearing a blindfold

___ Tying someone up/restraining someone

___ Being tied up or restrained

___ Talking dirty to someone

___ Having someone talk dirty to you

___ Role-playing

___ Wearing lingerie

___ Seeing your partner in lingerie

___ Other: _____

___ Other: _____

___ Other: _____

SEXUALITY AND AGING

"Although recognized as a fundamental driving force, human sexuality is frequently misunderstood and particularly in the elders, neglected," reports Kalra et. al. It leaves us asking many questions only to be determined by personal experience as we begin to age. How old is too old to have sex? How does aging affect having sex? What if you physically cannot have sex anymore? What if your partner's health does not allow them to be sexual anymore?

Though not enough research has been done, there is some reliable information that has been offered through various studies over the years. Kalra and colleagues report, "70% subjects perceived that their age negatively affected their sexuality," and "in every decade of life after 50" people felt their age began to affect their sexual desires "very much."

Despite the natural deterioration of health due to aging, about six in ten women over the age of 60 who are in committed relationships are sexually active. Meanwhile, women in their 60s and 70s report having sexual satisfaction levels similar to women in their 30s and forties. There is some credibility to the phrase, "you're only as old as you feel!"

However, despite feeling young at heart, aging does affect our physical health. The deterioration of muscle mass makes it more difficult to exercise, causing additional muscle mass to be lost over time. Our bodies store more fat, causing us to gain weight. Loss of bone density is also common, making it more likely to experience a fracture. Our hearts will also degenerate, slowing down blood flow. With a natural decline of water in our blood stream, the blood itself will decrease in volume over time, leading to slower circulation. These occurrences can lead to other health-related issues such as arthritis, which affects 31% of adults over age 65, causing pain and stiffness.

For men, one of the common side effects of aging is erectile dysfunction. This makes sense if we consider that blood flow decreases and men tend to have poorer circulation. As women age, especially with the onset of menopause, vaginal dryness is a common issue. This is also related to a decrease in blood flow. While many people are able to work around these issues, it is more difficult to address that the body is weaker and just does not operate the way it used to. When additional hardships such as pain, lethargy, and a decline in hormones are considered, it makes sense why people tend to have less sex as they age.

Therefore, as we age, it is essential that we reframe our concept of sex and recall the importance of intimacy. Joan Price, an expert on sexuality and aging, notes in her book *The Ultimate Guide to Sex After 50* that "*Aging affects sex in a gazillion ways: physical comfort, emotional needs, and what we need for sexual arousal and pleasure, to name a few*" (p. 13). Fortunately, if you have read the chapters on *Low Libido* and *Sexual Scripts,* you have learned that intimacy itself is more than just the act of sex. Intimacy is about expressing love, feeling loved, relieving stress, feeling connected to your partner, and feeling connected to yourself. While our bodies may not lend themselves to the acrobatics we used to be able to engage in, we are still able to experience intimacy in profoundly spiritual and erotic ways. *"We may need stronger or lighter stimulation now, a gentler or rougher touch, slower or faster pace, and lots more time. Sometimes we don't even know what we need,"* shares Price (p. 14). Rather than viewing our aging bodies as a burden, view it as an opportunity to fill a new box and learn additional ways to connect and experience pleasure.

Continued intimacy through aging may take some creativity, but people can have physical closeness by holding hands or doing Sensate Focus exercises, as outlined in the *Low Libido* chapter. While the focus may no longer be on orgasm, it does not mean intimacy is at a loss. There may also come a time when people have to rely on masturbation, due to their partner's incapacity or eventual passing. Read the chapter on *Masturbation* if you are ready to experience solo sex.

An elderly couple came to see me to help them process their own aging, mortality, and sexuality. Bob and Inga were both in their mid-80s and had been married for 46 years. They had both dealt with a series of health issues over the last decade. Inga was a breast cancer survivor, and she'd had a double mastectomy ten years ago. She was arthritic, had vaginal dryness, suffered from depression, and was overweight. Bob had his own set of health issues including erectile dysfunction due to an enlarged prostate and alcohol consumption, stiffness in his joints, and a previous heart attack in his early 70s. The couple had experienced a lot of life together including four children, the loss of a child, infidelity, cancer, surgeries, moves throughout the country, mental health issues, job lay-offs, their own business venture, and retirement.

They felt there were two presenting problems, as Bob and Inga each had different focal points. Bob was very focused on his inability to maintain erections, while Inga's focus was on her body image. The first two sessions were spent letting them both discuss their frustrations. They both felt they were inadequate in their own ways and had been using their energy to focus on these deficiencies. While they took turns complaining, they did not seem to be listening to one another, worrying about the other's concerns, or working towards a united goal.

After validating their personal concerns, I helped them refocus so we could discuss what had brought them to therapy. "Well, we want to have sex," Bob said matter-of-factly. I encouraged him to elaborate. "It just isn't like it used to be, and it's been almost three years. I don't know what Inga likes anymore, or what turns her on."

Inga muttered, "Neither do I," and averted her eyes, almost looking ashamed.

Turning to Inga, I questioned, "Does Bob like the same things he used to?" Slowly she connected what I was saying and responded, "Well, I guess neither of us like what we used to. Our bodies are just…different." It seemed like the couple was finally in a place to receive feedback.

We spent time talking about how their bodies, their sex life, and their daily lives had evolved over the years. We discussed sex being inclusive of various forms of intimacy, rather than viewing sex as an isolated event. This change in perspective allowed them to consider how their bodies were still serving them, rather than viewing them as burdens. They began to have more patience with one another, and with themselves, as they opened a new box to fill together.

During this time, Inga admitted to Bob that she had no desire to have intercourse due to her own body image issue, related to her mastectomy, and the vaginal dryness she experienced which caused her pain. "I don't care if you can't get an erection, Bobby," she also confided. While Bob still felt it was important to him to obtain an erection, at least for masturbation purposes, he realized his focus on erectile functioning was putting undue pressure on Inga to engage in an act she was no longer comfortable with or capable of doing. It took time for him to accept this though, and he needed a lot of reassurance from Inga that she still loved him and was attracted to him.

They both had to sort through the fact that the changes affecting their sex life were not personal, but were a natural part of aging. Coming together to process this allowed them to grieve as a couple what once had been, and to unite as partners about what was to come.

It is important to acknowledge and accept that our bodies change throughout the years. We naturally experience a loss of energy, mobility, and libido. Our bodies want us to slow down. Perhaps when it comes to sex and intimacy, it is our body's way of telling us to enjoy the process of intimacy, instead of rushing through it to accomplish an end goal. So where do we start with processing and accepting these changes? Our bodies have been changing for many years, so how do we help our minds catch up? The following exercises will help you to answer these questions.

■ EXERCISE ■

Answer the following questions by yourself and consider how sex and intimacy have changed for you, as it relates to aging. Take your time to thoughtfully process and reflect on each question. When you are ready, discuss the questions, and your answers, with your partner.

- How do you feel about your body now? How has it changed over the years? What could you do before that you can't do now? What can you do now, that you couldn't do before?

- How do you feel about your current intimate life? How has this changed over the years? What's better about it now?

What's easier? What's harder? What is difficult to accept about your current sex life?

- How have illnesses or mental health issues affected your sex life? Have you coped and accepted these changes, or are you still adjusting to them?

- What are your goals for sex and intimacy at this time? Is your partner in a place, physically and mentally, to help you achieve these goals? If not, how does this make you feel? Does it change your goals?

- What are your partner's goals for sex and intimacy at this time? Are you in a place, physically and mentally, to achieve these goals? If not, how does this make you feel?

▪ EXERCISE ▪

How do you stay connected and present in your body? Exercises, such as yoga and masturbation, can help improve muscle tone and flexibility as well as improve body image and self-esteem. Consider taking a yoga class at your local fitness center. Don't worry about your age or fitness ability because yoga can easily accommodate people with a variety of shapes, sizes, ages, and levels of mobility.

To learn more about solo sex, read the chapter on *Masturbation*. Both of these activities will help you center yourself as you practice being present within your body and finding a sense of acceptance and calmness.

▪ EXERCISE ▪

If you are in a relationship, the following tips can help you and your partner explore a new way to connect. Find a space big enough for you to lie down, such as your bed or a large couch.

What will help you to relax? Consider lighting candles, opening windows, or playing light music in the background. Then find a pillow to help provide support for your joints. I suggest investing in a Liberator Wedge, an angled, firm pillow offering support for your back, knees, and neck. The Liberator Wedge is a game-changer for many, and is advertised to provide "angles, elevations, curves, and motion that help people of all sizes find satisfying ways to connect with their partners."

Once you have found a comfortable position to lie down on your side, using your pillow or wedge to support you, have your partner get in a position where they are lying in front of you or behind you. Feel free to encourage them to use pillows to prop themselves up if necessary. Pillows can be used to support the head and neck, the knees and feet, or both. Lying side by side proves to be a comfortable position for both parties because you aren't putting your weight on one another, or having to hold your own weight, which is a common occurrence and strain in other sexual positions.

Feel your body pressing against one another. Focus on the warmth being generated between you two. Use your hands, moving them slowly up and down your partner's body. If this position and this state feel comforting, relaxing, and engaging, then stay in it as long as you like. There is no pressure to further engage or progress the intimacy between you.

However, if you find yourself getting aroused and turned on, feel free to continue, with your partner's permission. The person lying behind their partner can use their hands to stimulate the other person's genitals. They may continue to do this until the person reaches an orgasm. There is no pressure to orgasm, though, and having the genitals stimulated may be enough. If you want to, switch positions and roles.

SEXUALITY & ILLNESS

While aging does affect sexuality in a variety of ways, it is unlikely sex will lead to your mortality. The average age of mortality is 78.8 years in the United States. Men and women alike are most likely to die from heart disease, followed by cancer. Dying while having sex is directly related to cardiac arrest and is more likely if you do not exercise as you age. Many people experience illnesses and diseases that are not fatal, including cancer, diabetes, heart attack, and dementia.

What does life look like through illness? What about after? And just how does it affect sexuality? Read more about how you can engage sexually when undergoing chemotherapy and radiation, have just received a pacemaker, or are caring for a spouse that cannot even remember your first name.

There are times when both our minds and our bodies are affected by aging and disease. According to the Alzheimer's Association, 10% of adults over age 65 experience dementia and Alzheimer's, which affect a person's memory and decision-making skills. Both are typically diagnosed in aging individuals and have become the sixth leading cause of death in the United States.

Some people with dementia and Alzheimer's actually experience an increase in sexual desire. However, their memory is not fully intact and they may not be able to judge what is sexually appropriate. You should not have sex with someone who is not conscious of who you are, or what is happening. As a caretaker of someone who has dementia or Alzheimer's, this may be an additional loss to the many ways you feel you have already lost your partner. It can be difficult to reframe our view of intimacy and not see it as a loss or absence of something that once was. Finding a support group can be a helpful way to process the changes happening to your partner and how they are affecting you.

Approximately one in two men will experience a cancer diagnosis, while one in three women can expect the same. Cancer is the second most common cause of death in the United States, following heart disease. The National Cancer Institute estimates worldwide, "The number of new cancer cases per year is expected to rise to 23.6 million by 2030" from 14 million in 2012. Unfortunately, few doctors talk to their patients about sexuality, before, during, or after cancer treatment. While it may not be the number one thing on most people's minds when going through chemotherapy or radiation treatment, the prospect of losing one's sexuality is a real threat to many. With prostate cancer being the most common type of cancer for men, and breast cancer the most common type for women, it would be a disservice to neglect the subject of sexuality and cancer as it affects functioning and body image.

Some doctors, therapists, and cancer survivors are beginning to speak out and educate how cancer can, and does, alter a person's sexuality. These leaders addressing sexuality and cancer acknowledge the effects treatment has on the body and recognize that treatment also affects the cancer patient's partner. Depending on the severity of the cancer, and the type of treatment, people experience different changes to their body, including weight gain, hair loss, and loss of body parts or limbs.

I have met many women in my practice over the years who have struggled with, and overcome, breast cancer. Due to treatments like double mastectomies, radiation, and chemotherapy, women may experience fertility issues, weight gain, vaginal dryness, and overall low self-esteem.

Case study: Amy and Fred

When I first met Amy and her husband Fred it was for issues related to low libido. They were in their early forties when I met them and they had no desire for children. Amy was a nurse anesthesiologist and Fred was a poet and author. They saw me for about four months, and worked hard to reconnect sexually and physically. The couple worked on non-demand touch, as outlined in the *Low Libido* chapter, and Amy was able to find arousal in her breasts, while Fred realized that sex was not contingent on orgasms.

A few years later, I got an email from Amy requesting an appointment. I remembered the couple well, as they'd had quite the sense of humor. I presumed that, like many couples, they had gotten off track and were scheduling a tune-up. Still in good spirits when they arrived to my office, as they always were, Amy began, "so I have cancer."

Fred was more anxious this time around as he held Amy's hand and looked to her to speak first. She explained she had been diagnosed 12 weeks ago with breast cancer after finding a lump during a routine mammogram. Surgery was scheduled to have the lump removed, but due to concern about the size of the lump, doctors elected for a mastectomy. Amy's doctors then started her on radiation treatment.

"I was sitting at home two weeks ago, with drainage tubes, looking down at only one breast, when I emailed you. This is going to affect our sex life. It already has. Radiation has made me feel so tired and I still have four more weeks of treatment. I know that will get better, but every time I look down I'm reminded a piece of my sexuality is missing."

Amy elected to have reconstructive surgery and have a breast implant, but that surgery was scheduled for a few months from now. Regardless, she knew she would no longer have nipple sensation. Amy and Fred had decided they would rather seek professional support through this process, knowing sexually things would change throughout the course of her treatment. They knew the doctors were unlikely to discuss sex with them, although I did encourage Amy to advocate for herself and ask questions.

Throughout the course of Amy's cancer treatment and reconstructive surgery, the couple began with the talking exercise at the end of this chapter and did it several times in therapy. They realized each week their answers changed slightly as they adjusted to life during radiation, life without a breast, life after cancer, life post-reconstructive surgery, and life without a nipple. Amy admitted the most difficult part of the process for her was after reconstructive surgery. "Phantom nipple!" she exclaimed. "It's so odd, being at work, having an itch on my left nipple, which is always the worst at work, right? Having to itch your nipple," she laughed. "For a second, I feel normal needing to itch my nipple after all I've been through, until I realize I don't have one. Then I just feel crazy."

Fred felt he was most aware of how radiation had affected Amy's libido. He was reminded of where they had been four years ago, and that was scary for him because it was reminiscent of a time when they had discussed divorce due to lack of intimacy. The couple was grateful to have a space to process the boxes of their past, present, and future together.

Few couples seek out professional support during their journey with cancer; even fewer are offered such support. Sexuality is rarely discussed as part of the treatment process. This is slowly changing with cancer survivors advocating for more education from medical professionals.

Case study: Claude and Timothy

Sexuality and illness can be quite difficult to navigate. Claude, a retired man in his mid-70s, came to see me for support as he grieved his former sex life. He shared that his husband Timothy had been diagnosed with Parkinson's disease several years ago. As a couple they were able to deal with the diagnosis on their own for many years, since its progression was slow. However, Timothy was now experiencing severe symptoms and needed help with most daily activities, as his movement had been impaired. Claude still loved and cared for Timothy deeply but he was now a caretaker for his husband. "I just need your support, Kristen. How do I deal with this? How do we deal with this?"

Part of helping Claude process was allowing him the time and space to grieve. He missed the sexual intimacy he and Timothy had shared for so many years. Claude also needed a new box to fill with some support and fresh ideas. I encouraged him to think of how intimate the relationship was now. Initially, Claude wrinkled his nose at me and said, "I just told you there is no intimacy. It's all care-taking now."

I shot back, "That *is* intimacy, Claude." We spent time discussing what intimacy is and how vulnerable both Claude and Timothy were being in their current relationship, and how vulnerability can lead to intimacy.

I did acknowledge that what Claude was missing from his relationship was a sexual component. We spent time discussing ways to develop this component in a new way but had to account for Timothy's limitations. Eventually, Claude was also able to see his own limitations as an aging man too. While he was sad about losing the sexual intimacy he had been so familiar with over the years, he was able to grow other forms of intimacy with Timothy and process them in therapy.

Regardless of the type of illness you or your partner has experienced, it is important to take the time to learn, adapt, and process how your sex life has changed. You may need to find new ways to connect and be intimate. You may also need to take time to grieve the past before you can embrace the future.

■ EXERCISE ■

If you are still trying to process how illness and disease have affected your sexuality, address the following questions by journaling. If you have a partner to discuss them with, do so after you've processed the questions below. There's a second set of questions if you are the healthy partner who is supporting someone with an illness or disease.

If you are ill:

1. What does sexuality mean to you? How has this changed since becoming ill? How has it stayed the same?

2. What do you miss about intimacy with your partner?

3. In what kind of intimacy are you still able to engage? What kind of intimacy do you want to engage in?

If your partner is ill:

1. What does sexuality mean to you? How has this changed since your partner became ill? How has it stayed the same?

2. What do you miss about intimacy with your partner?

3. What kind of intimacy is your partner still able to engage in? Is this fulfilling? Why/why not?

▪ EXERCISE ▪

This is a simple guide to spooning, which can be done in bed, including a hospital bed. In general, spooning is ideal for anyone, including those enduring pain and arthritis because it can be done without exerting a lot of energy or pressure. People who have physical disabilities or changes in cognitive functioning can do this exercise, as well as the elderly. Spooning does not require any kind of mood-setting, unless the couple choose to create one. Background music and dimming the lights can be especially helpful if someone is in a hospital bed, as it can make the setting more intimate and be a reminder of life before illness, even if just for a few minutes. If someone is experiencing a change in cognitive functioning, it is best to maintain a recognizable environment and efforts should be made to keep the setting familiar.

Start by having the ill person lie down in the bed first. Help them get comfortable by surrounding them with pillows so they feel physically supported. Once they are comfortable, you can climb in bed behind them. Make yourself comfortable, then slide your body in to fit with theirs. Your front side should be connected with their backside. You can put your arm under your head so you can slide in closer. Feel your knees fitting into their legs. Smell your partner's neck and hair. Notice their breathing as you try to match their breath. Feel yourselves coming together as one. If you both feel comfortable, you can switch positions so your partner can slide into you. Use this time to feel close to one another.

MASTURBATION

Masturbation, or the act of touching your genitals, is often done with the intention of pleasure and experiencing an orgasmic release. There are a lot of positive reasons to masturbate: it alleviates stress, decreases the risk of prostate cancer and vaginal dryness, elevates mood, increases sexual confidence, improves body image, and is fun for many people! However, some people choose not to masturbate for a variety of reasons including religious beliefs, lack of libido, and pain. Masturbation may lead to complex emotions as well, such as feelings of guilt and shame, even if the act itself is enjoyable.

While people with penises typically masturbate at a higher frequency than those with a vagina, research confirms the majority of people have masturbated. However, research on masturbation is difficult to ascertain due to feelings of guilt and shame. Since most of the research relies on self-report, it is often unreliable because people lie and withhold information. Surveys and questionnaires that are completed anonymously are likely to have less bias than research that is done face-to-face. Most people are not comfortable talking about masturbation with a partner, let alone a researcher who is a complete stranger. Because of these challenges, it is difficult to know how much of the population has masturbated and how many people masturbate on a consistent basis.

Research aside, it is reasonable to assume that men masturbate at higher rates then women. Here's why: the penis is an external organ located outside the body, while the vagina is an internal organ (although the infamous clitoris is located outside the body and it goes unnoticed by many). Folks who have a penis must touch themselves every single day. They touch it when they go to the bathroom, when they wash themselves in the shower, and quickly learn that it feels good to touch this sensitive organ. People with vaginas however, could literally go their entire lives without touching themselves, by using toilet paper to wipe after using the bathroom and washing with a loofah in the shower. Based on physical anatomy, it is no wonder people with vaginas tend to masturbate at a later age (if ever).

So why should you masturbate? First of all, it is such a natural and innate thing babies do it in the womb. Yes, fetuses touch their genitals. Why? Because it feels good! In addition to feeling good, it is an overall stress reliever. Additionally, masturbation can be a key factor in your success to having an orgasm in partnered sex. This is especially true for women with vaginas. Knowing your body in the most intimate way possible will help you become more physically intimate with someone else. If you understand how to give yourself sexual pleasure, you can tell a partner how to give you pleasure.

I have discussed masturbation with many clients over the years. When men come to see me, they often question if they are masturbating *too much*. Similar to how it is nearly impossible to decipher what a sex addict is, aside from the client's personal opinion of the situation, the same is true regarding masturbation habits. What I *will* say is that if a person, regardless of genitalia, is masturbating to the point of causing sores, running to the bathroom at work due to urges, or always prefers solo play over partnered play, then the behavior may be problematic. This is more than just a habit if it is impacting your life in negative ways.

More often than not though, when I talk about masturbation with clients it is often with women coming to see me because they have never had an orgasm. They are often in their 20s or 30s and it is not surprising when they share they have never masturbated. They feel they are missing out on something in life after hearing their girlfriends brag about having multiple orgasms. These women may also feel pressure from their partner to climax.

Case study: Theresa

One of my most determined clients trying to achieve orgasm on her own was a woman named Theresa. While her story is similar to many in my office, her wit and motivation to change is unlike many. The first time Theresa came in to my office she sat down with an exasperated expression and looked at me. "So, *you're* gonna help me have an orgasm, huh? Well let's get to it." I stared at her, caught off guard by her comment, as she looked me over. "Well," I started, but she cut me off and dove right in. "Look I know it's all in my noggin, so I need your help to shake things up a bit," she declared as she tapped the side of her head with her finger.

Unlike many of the young women I see, Theresa was in her late 60s. She had run a local boutique for over three decades and always came to therapy adorned with some of her prized jewels. Widowed five years ago, Theresa had lived a rich life with her husband Russell, an accountant, until he died from a heart attack. They had two children together, both adults living on their own now. "We lived a nice life, you know? The sex was fine too. Just fine. Never good, but fine."

Upon her husband's death, Theresa took the liberty to explore her own sexuality. "I always knew I was bisexual. Russell did too. I never did anything about it so it wasn't much of a conversation." Theresa continued, sharing that orgasms had never been a priority in her sex life with Russell. She was content having sex to make Russell happy. However, when she met Susanne six months ago, she began to feel differently. Suddenly, Theresa felt like she had been missing out on a carnal experience. "It's just totally different, feeling a woman have an orgasm, and realizing you can't share in that experience."

Our work was cut out for us, but Theresa was determined to have an orgasm with Susanne and share in the delight. We had a lot to discuss and boxes to unpack about Theresa's sexual dynamics from her marriage to Russell, including communication issues, sexual positioning, and a lack of clitoral stimulation. Like many women, sex had become something on her to-do list, rather than an intimate and shared experience. This was in part due to the fact that she was not experiencing sexual pleasure with her spouse. In addition, Theresa was dealing with her own internalized homophobia since embracing her bisexuality and entering into a relationship with Susanne. While some of the boxes in Theresa's history were messy and complicated, she was focused and determined to organize them. She was engaged in sessions and generally self-aware.

Despite how she started her first session, Theresa was very open to feedback, which made it easy and comfortable to challenge her when she was feeling stuck. Due to her determination, Theresa followed through with her homework and did daily breathing and meditation exercises to practice being present in her own body. She also tried masturbating, something she had not attempted to do since she was in her 20s because it had been "pointless" and "time consuming." While the process was not as quick as she had hoped, four months after starting therapy Theresa walked into my office and sat down at the edge of the couch, a smile beaming from ear to ear, and said, "I did it. My first orgasm. All by myself, and Susanne was there to watch." I smiled back at her and then she began to laugh until she began to sob. It was an opportunity to hold space and validate her emotional state while she collected her thoughts. When she was ready, she let out one more sob followed by a smirk. "That was kind of like an orgasm too, ya know? It's just this build-up and then it all comes out and afterwards you experience this release." Theresa was grateful she could now understand and describe the euphoria she had experienced. She scheduled a few more sessions as she learned how to replicate her own sexual bliss, but within a month she was ready to just live and experience this newfound ecstasy and was done processing it.

You can experience sexual bliss too. If you have never masturbated, you might be unsure where to start. You might even have thoughts that masturbating is weird or gross. While the exercises following this chapter are a great place to start becoming comfortable with your body and masturbation, there are entire books written on this topic too. If you want further reading, I frequently recommend *Becoming Cliterate* by Dr. Laurie Mintz and *The Elusive Orgasm* by Dr. Vivienne Cass, both geared at people with vaginas.

■ EXERCISE ■

If you have never masturbated, start by touching yourself, right on your bare-naked legs. To do this intentionally, first find a comfortable position. You may choose to lie down on your bed, sit on the floor, or curl up in a chair. Next, select your favorite lotion and rub a dollop onto your hands. Rub your hands together and bring them up to your nose. Close your eyes and breath in the smell of the lotion. What does it remind you of? How does it make you feel?

When you are ready, open your eyes and slowly rub the lotion onto your legs. Slow the process down and actually feel what is happening to your body. Focus on the sensations. Is the lotion cool? Calming? Are you still focused on how it smells? Or are you focusing on how your legs feel in this moment? Are you relaxed or tense? Pay attention to your body. Do this exercise several times so you can truly soak up the sensation of putting on the lotion. Once you are comfortable putting it on your legs, try rubbing it onto other parts of your body, such as your stomach and buttocks.

You could try this exercise with other things as well, such as feeling the water pressure on your body while in the shower, the suds on your body as you wash your hair or face, and the stark difference while drying off with a towel. The point is to slow down your routine, and hopefully try something a little outside of it too, so you can focus on your body's sensations.

■ EXERCISE ■

Once you have mastered the first exercise, you can try this one. This time you will engage in genital touching. Make sure you are in a comfortable and private place. Decide what will help you feel most relaxed. Do you want music on in the background? No noise at all? Are your pillows supportive or are you thinking about how lumpy they are? Try to eliminate as many distractions as you can.

When you are ready, slowly undress yourself. Notice how it feels to remove your clothes. Pay attention to the air when it hits your skin. Close your eyes, take a deep breath, and move into your desired position. You may choose to sit on the floor, lie in your bed, or relax in the bathtub. Take another deep breath and notice your body as it sinks into the ground. Focus on your breath and relax your body.

When you are ready, take your hand and gently rub it over your skin. Touch your arm, your thigh, your stomach. Notice how it feels and how soft your skin is. Consider how capable your body is as it supports your weight, the ability of your hands to change pressure, and your lungs to breath at a pace you set. As you come into your body's wonderment, slowly move your hand down to your genitals. Use a lubricant if that will help you feel more comfortable. Slowly massage the genitals, noticing the different textures and how they feel.

How are *you* feeling? Check in with yourself. Slow your breath again if you need to. The goal of this exercise is not to have an orgasm, but to become familiar with your most intimate self. Continue to touch and explore your genitals for as long as you feel comfortable. This should be a pleasurable experience. If you start to get a cramp in your hand or your back, try changing positions or consider ending the exercise. This is not about how long you can touch yourself, it is about quality and creating a pleasurable experience free of anxiety and judgment.

When you are ready to stop the exercise, slowly move your hands back to your stomach, thighs, and arms. Continue to pace your breathing. When you are ready, slowly position your body upright. Again, take a deep breath as you slowly open your eyes and come back to the present moment. Notice your surroundings and let yourself slowly adjust to the four walls around you. Breathe in all of your surroundings. When you are ready, you can climb into bed and sleep, take a shower and start your day, or move back into your routine.

PHYSICAL DISABILITY

A person is physically disabled when they have a physical impairment in functioning, putting limits on daily activity and living. The World Health Organization estimates, throughout the world, nearly one billion people have some sort of disability. The 15% of the population affected by physical and cognitive disabilities may have been born with impairments or may have developed them later in life.

Due to chronic disease and health issues, physical disabilities are often seen in the aging and elderly. Because people are living longer than ever before, physical disabilities are becoming more prominent. It is worthwhile to note that the World Health Organization also recognizes, "Disability is now understood to be a human rights issue. People are disabled by society, not just by their bodies."

Due to barriers to transportation, health care access, and job opportunities, people with disabilities are often discriminated against. This includes not being seen as sexual beings. Free expression of sexuality is a basic human right, so when others do not see people with disabilities as sexual beings, they are being denied part of their basic functioning. This is an issue for people with physical disabilities at the doctor, with a caretaker, while dating, and when it comes to reproductive rights.

Activities, sexual and otherwise, may also look different depending how many spoons a person has left to work with—not actual spoons, just the theoretical kind. Christine Miserandino named the spoon theory in 2003 in an essay about living with lupus. The concept is that people wake up in the morning with a certain number of spoons each day. For each activity they engage in, they lose a spoon. If they exert too much energy, physical or mental, then they may lose multiple spoons at a time, or use spoons that had been reserved for the following day. If this occurs, they may not have enough energy to engage in activities the next day because they are out of spoons. While sleep often helps fill the reserve again, this is not always true and varies greatly by the person, the activity, and the disability. Sex and intimacy do require spoons.

People with disabilities may also struggle with dating because they are seen for their disability first, before their personality and appearance. They are often asked *how* they can have sex if they are in a wheelchair or paralyzed. While there may be some additional considerations, people with physical disabilities can have sex and engage in intimacy just like someone who is able-bodied. What might be different is sexual positioning, mobility, or erogenous zones (areas that feel pleasurable to touch).

Examples of pleasure for someone with a disability are as vast as the number of people with disabilities. A person who is paraplegic might need assistance moving from their wheelchair to the bed and getting into a comfortable position, using pillows for stability, and may find having their ears massaged a sexual turn-on. However, there are many able-bodied people who also enjoy being touched in this erogenous zone.

Fortunately, more people with physical disabilities are speaking out and creating awareness about their intimate needs. This has led to sexual products, resources, books, and websites that cater just to those with disabilities. This increase in awareness has led to the normalization and visibility of people with disabilities and acknowledges their sexual wants and needs.

Over the years, I have worked with many individuals and couples with disabilities. One of my favorite success stories was a man with muscular dystrophy who was wheelchair bound. He was married with two children, and reported regular intimacy with his spouse. However, he had struggled with erectile dysfunction for many years and shared he was unable to obtain an erection during times of intimacy. After just one session together, and offering him a surplus of resources and exercises, he emailed me a few weeks later to let me know that for the first time in nearly ten years he had been able to achieve an erection and have an orgasm with his wife.

Case study: Antonio

A young black man, Antonio, came to see me three years after suffering from a spinal cord injury resulting from a motorcycle accident. In a matter of seconds, Antonio had become one of 250,000 people in the United States with a spinal cord injury. Antonio was only 25 at the time of his accident and he had gone through a long road of recovery over the last few years, filled with guilt and grief, as he learned how his body now functioned.

The motorcycle accident caused a spinal cord injury, leaving Antonio paralyzed. Through extensive physical therapy, Antonio was able to live alone, control a wheelchair, and even drive a car that had special adaptations. Things he no longer had control over, which made him self-conscious, were his bladder and bowel movements, and weak hand functioning. When he came to see me, he wanted to work on a variety of issues, which included consistent masturbation techniques, dating, and discussing his anxieties about making love to a woman. He admitted, "I haven't had a sexual encounter, with myself or anyone else, in over three years. It's taken me a long time to know my body again, but my sexuality seems disconnected to my body."

I spent a lot of time helping Antonio reorganize the contents of his box that defined what sexuality was to him. He explored body image issues, the trauma his body endured, treatment of his body by medical staff, how to communicate his sexual wants and needs, and learning about his own spoon reserve.

A resource that was very useful for Antonio was the book, *The Ultimate Guide to Sex and Disability,* which helped him have a better understanding of his body, fatigue, positioning, and self-image. While reading this resource, Antonio discussed his thoughts and feelings as he reflected on the literature during therapy.

Because Antonio was struggling with limited mobility plus weak bladder and bowel control, we also focused on masturbation techniques. The intention was that many of these techniques would be replicable in the bedroom with another person. Simple techniques helped Antonio navigate these issues, create confidence, and also satisfy sexual needs. We discussed eliminating his bladder and bowel before engaging in sexual behavior. Eliminating waste from his body decreased the chances of him experiencing an issue he felt was embarrassing. Antonio also used a Liberator waterproof blanket, which would soak up any fluid secretions he might eliminate, including ejaculate fluid. Antonio liked the blanket so much he also purchased a Liberator Wedge so he could position himself more comfortably in bed while masturbating.

To improve his masturbation technique, he utilized ideas from the *Pleasurable* resource guide by MacHattie and Naphtali, and bought a cuff link to help maximize the motor functions in his hands. The cuff would secure around his hand, and an elastic strap would attach to something secure (for him it was either his wheelchair or a bedpost) so his hand could then be used to touch the genitals.

Something that changed for Antonio's sexual functioning, that he had to process, was that he could not readily obtain an erection the way he used to. He could not feel himself having a genital orgasm because of his injury. He could see that he had ejaculated, but he could not feel anything happening. Antonio mourned this, fearful he would never have an orgasm again, but grateful he could still ejaculate. Over time, and with guidance, he also discovered great pleasure in other erogenous zones.

As Antonio gained confidence opening the box to discuss his sexuality in sessions and having successes at home with masturbation, he decided to create a profile on a popular dating site. He did this while in therapy so he could have support during the dating process. Antonio had not dated anyone in several years and had only had one long-term relationship from college. There was fear he would be rejected due to his disability. But within a few months, Antonio had gone on several dates and had been dating one woman for the last six weeks. He was hopeful it would turn into a long-term relationship and he reported that the sex was great.

If you have a physical disability, it is important to remember that your disability does not strip you of your sexuality. If you acquired a disability later in life, you may have to adapt and adjust to how your body functions now without constantly comparing it to what your body used to be able to do. It is okay to grieve and process this change. In addition, you may discover new sensations and sexual abilities that you didn't previously acknowledge or enjoy, such as nipple sensation. The following exercises are intended to help you do just that.

▪ EXERCISE ▪

Perhaps you were born with a physical disability. Perhaps you acquired one later in life. Perhaps it affects your mobility. Perhaps it causes you chronic pain. Regardless, you are a sexual being. Perhaps you are reading this because you are just now realizing it, just now embracing it, or just coming to terms with yourself as a sexual being who also happens to have a disability. As you move forward merging those identities, consider the following questions, so long as you have enough spoons to process them. If not, feel free to come back to the questions later, or do them one at a time. You may choose to just think about the questions, journal and write about them, or talk through them with your therapist.

1. How do you view your body as sexual, despite your disability?

2. How does your sexuality and disability affect you emotionally?

3. Has anyone else ever viewed you as non-sexual because of your disability? What happened? How did this feel?

4. Has someone sexualized you because of your disability? What happened? How did this feel?

5. What do you value most about your body?

6. What do you struggle with most about your physical limitations?

7. How do you manage pain?

8. Do you manage your spoons? How do you manage spoons with sexual activity?

9. What is your biggest fear about being intimate and having a disability? If you have a partner, have you discussed these fears with them?

10. What do you value most about sex and intimacy?

■ EXERCISE ■

If you feel comfortable in your body, but are struggling with society's definition of sex and orgasm, this exercise is for you. The body is filled with 100 billion nerve cells, containing many erogenous zones. While the genitals and nipples are often the first erogenous zones people think of, there are many more, including earlobes, fingers, eyelids, and even the back of your knees. How do you discover new erogenous zones on your body?

Start by making sure you have enough spoons to do this exercise. You can do this exercise alone or with a partner. You will likely have to do this exercise multiple times, with continued patience, before experiencing the results you are looking for. Make yourself physically comfortable by either sitting or lying down. Perhaps you want to light a candle, dim the lights, or play some music in the background. When you are ready, think of a sexual fantasy. If you need help with this, review the *Fantasy* chapter. Notice what is happening to your body as you think about your fantasy. Pay attention to your breathing, to your heart rate, and notice the blood flowing through your body. Notice if your ears are starting to get hot or if your muscles are tensing. Where do you feel yourself getting aroused? As you focus on your fantasy, and your body, start to think yourself into an orgasm. Imagine your muscles spasming and your nerves tingling.

When you are ready, take a deep breath and center yourself. Slowly open your eyes. How is your body feeling? Were you able to stay focused or were there too many distractions? Were you able to dream up a sexual fantasy?

Again, this exercise may need to be done several times before you start to notice the effect on your body. If you have a partner, try doing this exercise alone and then with your partner to see what the noticeable differences are.

PREGNANCY AND SEX

According to the World Health Organization, 211 million pregnancies occur annually, with about 4 million of those taking place in the United States. Of those, about 123 million are planned pregnancies, while the other 87 million are unintentional. The use of contraceptives has not only reduced unintended pregnancies, but has also reduced the number of children women do have as they engage in more intentional family planning. Worldwide, the average woman had 4.97 children in the 1960s, but currently only 2.69. This is in part due to the rising costs of having children, society accepting the choice not to procreate, and a focus on career choices over family.

For women who are pregnant and carry to full term, they will experience three trimesters of pregnancy. The first trimester occurs from weeks 0–13, and includes the most important stages of development as the fetus develops major organs. It is also when women are most likely to have a miscarriage or lose the pregnancy before the 20th week, which happens to about one in four pregnancies. Many women who have a miscarriage experience it so early on that they may not even realize they were pregnant. The first trimester is also when women experience the most uncomfortable symptoms of pregnancy, including morning sickness (nausea), fatigue, breast tenderness, cramps, and decreased libido. Of course, every person is different, and some women will experience all of these side effects while others may not have any.

If the fetus continues to develop, women will enter into the second trimester from weeks 14–26, sometimes referred to as the "honeymoon period." Typically during this time pregnancy symptoms start to subdue and women are likely to get their sex drive back! The body is visibly showing signs of pregnancy, which may cause back pain from the additional weight gain. The fetus should now have an audible heartbeat and develop an umbilical cord. It is also possible to find out the sex of the baby at the 20-week appointment.

During the final trimester, weeks 27–40, people are often excited, scared, and anxious to meet their growing baby. Pregnancy symptoms may become more uncomfortable due to weight gain, shortness of breath, and incontinence. It may be more difficult to sleep or sit comfortably in these final weeks.

For many people, trying to get pregnant is part of the fun. However, it can feel mechanical when tracking periods, ovulation, and cervical fluids. Sex becomes scheduled and your partner's ejaculation is crucial. You may forego your own orgasms because you have a goal in mind, and sexual pleasure is not it. This process can be stressful and taxing on a couple. It is best to try to enjoy the process and alleviate as much pressure as possible.

Schedule an appointment with your doctor if you are having difficulty conceiving after the first year of trying. When trying to conceive is filled with stress, it removes aspects of intimacy and can make it difficult to reestablish a fun and carefree sex life.

Once you have become pregnant, keep having sex! Unless a doctor directs you otherwise, having sex while pregnant is completely safe. The fetus is protected within the uterus and the cervix forms a mucous plug to prevent against infection. Many women find that sex is more pleasurable during pregnancy because the body naturally has increased blood flow, and some of that goes directly to the genitals, which can increase arousal. If you have a normal pregnancy you can actually have intercourse up until your water breaks. If you do not want to have intercourse, because your doctor says you cannot or you are uncomfortable with your body and the idea of having sex, you can find other ways to be intimate with your partner. See the exercises in the chapters on *Low Libido, Sexual Scripts,* and *Kink* for additional ideas.

After giving birth, women may experience a whole new set of post-pregnancy symptoms including bleeding, post-partum depression, vaginal dryness, build-up of scar tissue, and pelvic pain. Many of these symptoms are related to the drastic change in hormones, specifically a drop in estrogen and an increase in oxytocin. Vaginal dryness may continue throughout the duration of breastfeeding.

After giving birth, it is typically recommended to wait six to eight weeks before having intercourse. This gives the body several weeks to heal from tearing that may have occurred during a vaginal birth, and to ensure the cervix is no longer dilated. Remember, there are many additional ways to be intimate with a partner that do not include vaginal intercourse.

Case study: Kitty and Mark

A couple in their mid-30s came to see me about six months after having their first baby. Kitty and Mark had been together for eight years and married for three. After the baby, Kitty was able to negotiate her position at the bank to work remotely from home. Mark continued his work as a youth pastor at their local church. Both came from a religious background and neither had previous sexual partners before getting married to each other. Having an active sex life had been a struggle for Kitty since their marriage began, but having a baby compounded it.

"Sex has always been uncomfortable for me. I'm angry at the church," she said firmly before darting her eyes towards Mark. He nodded in acknowledgement and she continued. "I was always told that sex was for marriage, so I waited and waited. I don't regret waiting. What I regret is that sex was painted as this picture, something magical you do with your spouse, but completely forbidden before marriage. Well, it hasn't been magical, and I'm angry no one told me that. You don't just go from saving yourself for over 30 years to just having sex freely and willy-nilly."

This was a story I had heard from many previous clients. While there was value in their religious beliefs, the only sex education they received was *don't have it*. When couples from religious backgrounds start having sex, they may experience feelings of guilt, shame, and confusion. They may have an entire box filled with negative messages about sex, and they need to throw away this box and build a new one.

Kitty actually felt she had made a lot of progress during the first two years of marriage to become more comfortable sexually, and had worked through a lot of her own religious guilt.

Mark agreed. He also admitted the adjustment had been easier for him as he experienced a different kind of pressure than Kitty had growing up in the church. Mark found sex extremely pleasurable beginning the night they consummated their marriage. "Sex was awkward at first, figuring out what goes where and feeling self-conscious about what I was doing, but it's always been pleasurable for me." Two years into the marriage, they had negotiated having sex weekly but rarely discussed it. The act was mechanical.

Once Kitty became pregnant, she decided she did not want to have sex. She was able to utilize the pregnancy as an avoidance technique for nine months, and it worked. Unfortunately, after the birth of the baby, it compounded the couple's issues even more. Now, in addition to having guilt and shame connected to intercourse, Kitty was also struggling with pain from intercourse due to the buildup of scar tissue from the vaginal birth. When they started therapy, she was still breastfeeding as well, which was causing vaginal dryness and had made her nipples so cracked and dry she was uninterested in engaging in nipple play.

Mark was patient but also frustrated. He quite enjoyed sex with his wife and he found it difficult to understand a perspective he couldn't relate to. It had left him feeling unsure how to support his wife physically or emotionally and he felt like he was "walking on eggshells" anytime he tried to address the subject.

Despite this, it was actually Kitty who suggested going to sex therapy. Mark was hesitant at first, feeling they should seek pastoral counseling, but out of desperation, agreed to give it a try. They did not know how to navigate the conversation on their own, and after their first couples session they both agreed they had come to the right place. They were looking for direct discussion and tangible resolutions.

To address or rule out any medical issues, Kitty was encouraged to make an appointment with a specialist to see how her scar tissue was healing and if she was experiencing any infections. The couple were also encouraged to do an exercise from the *Communication* chapter so they would feel more comfortable talking about sex. This also helped them understand how each of their backgrounds influenced their views on sexual intercourse and sexuality.

After going to a specialist, Kitty came back to our next appointment with some enlightening, albeit frustrating, information.

She was informed that the obstetrician who delivered the baby had given her a "husband stitch." While sometimes done with a patient's consent, doctors will add an additional stitch after natural tearing during childbirth so the vaginal opening is literally tighter and smaller. It has been believed the doctor is doing the husband a favor after a natural childbirth and thus it has gotten the nickname the "husband stitch." Kitty reports she did not ask for an additional stitch and had she not seen a specialist she never would have known. Mark denied knowing this information prior to the most recent doctor appointment, and was shocked.

As suspected, Kitty did still have scar tissue build-up as well. Unfortunately, it seemed the scar tissue was not healing ideally, so she was experiencing tightness as her muscles tensed instead of relaxing. This tensing was increasing the vaginal pain Kitty felt with intercourse, causing her anxiety and making her tense her body, as well as her pelvic floor muscles, causing even more pain.

It was a lot to unpack. Kitty not only felt anger towards her religious community, but now she felt angry towards her medical team too.

Mark's patience was paramount in supporting Kitty's experience because it offered validation and removed undue pressure. We spent time redefining intimacy, as I have with many clients regarding sexuality issues. This also helped alleviate some of the pressure Kitty was feeling and gave her time to focus on healing her body in a physical sense, while working on healing emotionally in therapy.

The couple agreed to remove intercourse from their sexual menu at this time. It was different than when Kitty was pregnant, at which time she was admittedly avoiding sex. This was a deliberate conversation the couple had and they agreed to foster communication and intimacy in other ways.

It is recommended that you discuss sex in an open and honest way while pregnant or after giving birth. It is probable that you are comfortable having sex, until you aren't. A person's body changes a lot during pregnancy and after childbirth. Many people have an image of what an ideal pregnancy looks like, and create birthing plans so they can have an enriching birthing experience. Unfortunately, things do not always go as planned. Avoiding sex completely will not help you or your partner navigate intimacy before or after the baby arrives. The exercises that follow offer conversations and physical exercises to do while pregnant and/ or after delivery so you can have an ideal experience pre- and post-partum.

■ EXERCISE ■

Below are a series of questions to consider during your pregnancy journey, or post-partum. You could journal about them, discuss them in therapy, and then talk them through with your partner. This exercise is not to find solutions or fix problems, but serves as a way to reflect on all of the changes your body has endured.

1. How do you feel about your body right now? Are you embracing your body's changes? Are you in pain? Is this pain new? How do you feel in your clothes? How do you feel naked?

2. How does touch from your partner feel? Is it the same? Different? Are you more sensitive? Less sensitive? Do you invite and welcome touch or avoid it?

3. How does penetration feel? Is it the same? Does it feel tighter? Are you experiencing any pain with intercourse? Is this pain new or different?

4. Are there sexual positions you used to be able to do that are now difficult or uncomfortable? Are you able to change positions to alleviate pain or discomfort? If so, what are they?

▪ EXERCISE ▪

During pregnancy, it is vital to massage the perineum, particularly the last few weeks of your pregnancy. This intentional massage is done to loosen the muscles between the vaginal opening and the anus to help prevent tearing or an episiotomy. If tearing like this occurs, stitches will be required. While some tearing is common, it may be preventable. After delivery, many women develop scar tissue, sometimes from these stiches and particularly after having a vaginal birth, as the vaginal tissue heals. Scar tissue in the vulvar and vaginal region might result in lack of blood circulation and blocked nerve endings, resulting in pain to the touch.

So how do you massage your perineum while pregnant? How do you massage scar tissue post-partum to prevent the tissue from becoming tight and hard? For both, follow the steps below. You may choose to do this in a quiet room, where you can lay down or stretch out comfortably. Find a position that works for you and feel free to change positions if it works today but not tomorrow. You may choose to do the perineal massage yourself or have a partner do it for you.

- Wash your hands and trim your nails.
- Get comfortable. Take a deep breath and allow your body to relax.
- Use a gel made for perineal massage and post-partum recovery to aid in the massage. It will make the massage easier and hydrate the skin. Re-apply if you need more gel during the massage.
- Using your fingers, massage in a circular motion from the opening of the vagina to the opening of the anus. Be sure to massage the tender skin in between.

- Insert your thumb about an inch into the vaginal canal and use gentle pressure to massage the vaginal walls, moving your thumb back and forth. You should also use your thumb to push down towards the anus and stretch the vaginal wall this way.

- Do this for 5 minutes each day to prevent tearing (about six weeks before childbirth) and to help healing (starting six weeks after childbirth).

▪ EXERCISE ▪

Unless noted by your doctor, you can safely have oral sex or penile-vaginal intercourse throughout your pregnancy. Just make sure no air is blown into the vagina during oral sex, and keep your partner's weight off of your stomach. After childbirth, it is recommended to wait six to eight weeks before attempting intercourse again. You can talk to your doctor more about this. During and after pregnancy, some positions may be more comfortable than others, depending on your experience. While it is always an option to engage in other forms of intimacy, here are some positioning tips for engaging in penile-vaginal intercourse:

- The V: While laying on your side, spread your legs. Have your partner lay on their side, facing you. Your lower legs may touch. Have him insert his penis into the vaginal canal and put his top leg between your legs to offer support.

- The Edge: Lie on your back and slide your pelvis to edge of bed. Spread your legs apart. You may wish to use a pillow under your hips to raise your pelvis slightly. Have your partner stand at the end of the bed and position himself in a way to insert his penis into your vagina.

- The Top: Your partner should be lying down on his back. Spread your legs apart and position yourself so you are on top of him. This gives you greater control over insertion and depth. If you are pregnant, this also may be more comfortable because your belly is not in the way of insertion.

- The Behind: Lie down on your side. Have your partner lay down on his side behind you, in a spooning position. Have him insert his penis. You may wish to use his hand, your hand, or a toy for clitoral stimulation.

SEXUALLY TRANSMITTED INFECTIONS AND STDS

Sexually transmitted infections and diseases sound scary, and carry lots of stigma, but what are they and how can you still date and be sexual if you have one? A sexually transmitted infection (STI) is caused by bacteria. A sexually transmitted disease (STD) is caused by a virus. STIs may also be caused by parasites, such as pubic lice. It has become common practice to refer to them all as STIs.

While the words "sexual transmission" indicate bacteria and viruses are obtained via sexual activity, there are several ways to contract STIs including through pregnancy, childbirth, and sharing needles. Transmission occurs from being exposed to one of four fluids: blood, vaginal secretions, ejaculate fluid, and breast milk. However, there are exceptions such as with pubic lice, which is contracted without any fluids, and oral herpes, which is often contracted from parent to child via innocent kisses or sharing drinks.

There are 27 different known infections for STIs and STDs. The most common bacterial infections are chlamydia, gonorrhea, and syphilis. The most common diseases are herpes, human immuno-deficiency virus (HIV), and human papillomavirus (HPV).

Approximately one in four youth ages 15–24 will contract an STI. STIs frequently are asymptomatic, meaning a person who has contracted one will not experience any symptoms. The problem is that, if left untreated, they can still have severe consequences from lesions to pelvic inflammatory disease (PID). Oftentimes, the consequences are harsher for women than for men, and the Centers for Disease Control and Prevention (CDC) estimates untreated infections and diseases leave approximately 20,000 women infertile each year. Infection may increase for people who have new or multiple sexual partners.

Despite medical interventions and the use of condoms, sexually transmitted infections and diseases seem to be on the rise. The CDC estimates a contributing factor to the rise in STIs is funding cuts. These cuts affect statewide and local programs resulting in fewer staff, shorter clinic hours where people get tested and receive treatment, and even clinics shutting down completely. Part of encouraging people to get tested for STIs is to normalize the conversation, have *easier* access to testing and treatment, and use condoms or dental dams to prevent transmission.

What if you become one of the 25% of Americans living with an incurable STD? Many people will feel embarrassed and angry. How did you get it? Who gave it to you? How will you tell your partner? Did your partner cheat on you? Will you ever date again? Feelings of betrayal, guilt, and worthlessness may overcome you. Perhaps you've already processed the news of contraction, or perhaps you are reading this to begin processing this informa-tion. Wherever you are at with acknowledging and accepting, you are now one of millions living with an STD. Start with a deep breath. You are one of millions and you are still special, unique and worthy. Your future is still yours to live, however you decide to navigate it.

Case study: Marjorie

A woman named Marjorie came to see me after her recent herpes diagnosis. Marjorie was a 24-year-old pansexual woman. She had been dating her girlfriend Laura on and off for the last three years. During an "off" period, Marjorie had spent time with someone else, a longtime friend for whom she had always possessed feelings. A few weeks after visiting her friend, who lived in another state, she realized she wanted to truly make the relationship with Laura work. She also realized something was "different" on her vulva: a small red blister.

Marjorie immediately made an appointment with her gynecologist to have it examined. "I was crying and shaking as they did the blood draw. I was so confused and embarrassed," she told me. The results came back positive for herpes (HSV-2) and chlamydia. She immediately took the medication to treat the chlamydia and got a medication to treat the herpes symptoms. However, "It was only two weeks ago. I didn't know what to do. I still don't. So I made an appointment with you," she confided, her eyes filling up with tears as she looked to me for solace and guidance.

During her session, Marjorie confided she had not told Laura yet, and her way of dealing with things was to put the box in a corner and to avoid sex completely. She was feeling scared, hurt, and embarrassed, and she didn't want Laura to feel this way too. "I should probably just break up with her. She deserves better. I should just be alone. She knows I'm acting weird."

I gave Marjorie a safe space to vent and process her emotions. I also educated her on living with the herpes virus, since over 15% of people in the United States between the ages of 14 and

49 also have the disease. We also discussed rates of transmission and preventative measures.

Marjorie was not sure when, or how, to tell Laura, but she knew she needed to talk to her friend with whom she'd had the sexual encounter a few weeks prior. Calling him on the phone made the most sense due to proximity, and Marjorie agreed to do that before our next session. The phone call was difficult, she reported, but also a relief.

During the conversation, she decided to end the friendship as well. Despite her previous feelings for her friend, this experience had felt like a betrayal to her, although he denied being privy to having an STI. She also wanted to focus on her relationship with Laura, if it was salvageable, once she confessed she had contracted herpes. After the phone call Marjorie felt she could now focus on how to tell Laura and how to rebuild the trust she was undoubtedly going to break.

The following session, Marjorie decided it would be best to bring Laura with her to an appointment. She decided telling Laura in a therapeutic setting would give her the courage to say everything and would provide them both with the support they needed. When Laura came to the session, she was obviously nervous, unsure why Marjorie had brought her to a sex therapist's office.

Marjorie took a deep breath and then, through tears, confessed everything to Laura. Laura turned away, clearly shocked at everything Marjorie had just told her. She had known about Marjorie's rendezvous with her friend, which lessened the blow, but it did not change any of the facts.

"How are you feeling Laura?" I asked, trying not to press but wanting to check in. Snapping out of her shock, Laura looked at me and pursed her lips before responding, "Sad." Tears filled her eyes as she turned her body towards Marjorie and took her hands. "I'm sad you felt you couldn't share this with me, Marge.

I'm sad you've been going through this alone. I'm sad you thought I would leave you over this."

Tears spilled from Marjorie's eyes as she expressed both gratitude and more guilt. Laura attended the next few sessions with Marjorie so they could discuss their relationship, the herpes diagnosis, and their communication skills. Laura agreed to get tested and was pleased to find the results were negative. They also talked about rebuilding trust and how to move forward with their relationship and their sex life as they navigated Marjorie's herpes diagnosis.

Many people feel guilt the same way Marjorie did. They feel like they did something wrong, or they did something to deserve an STI. We do not shame people for having a cold, or ask how they got it or whom they've been kissing lately. We just assume it is part of life. However, we do things to prevent colds such as washing our hands, sneezing into a tissue, and getting a yearly physical exam. Yes Means Test, a website that will help you find a testing clinic nearest you, declares, "Getting an STD is human, it's normal. So why are we still uncomfortable talking about it? Especially when we can do something about it." This does not mean everyone will get an STI and, as with colds, we can take preventative measures to avoid contraction. Yet even the best of us might get one. We can do things to prevent STIs such as minimizing our sexual partners, using a latex condom or dental dam as a barrier, and getting tested regularly. The exercises below will help you have the courage to get tested and help you tell your partner if you have a positive result.

■ EXERCISE ■

Have you ever been tested for a sexually transmitted disease or infection? Did you know you can often get tested for free? Did you know free tests typically only test for chlamydia and gonorrhea?

Did you know that if you test positive, treatment is often free too? Did you know the results are confidential? Did you know you have to make a doctor appointment to request a full screening to be tested for all infections and diseases? Did you know a full screening often includes a urine test, blood test, and culture exam? Did you know that a standard physical or gynecological exam does not include testing and you must request it? Did you know there are at-home test kits to do your own STI screenings?

Now that you know all about getting tested, what are you waiting for? You can schedule an appointment with your doctor or go to your local Planned Parenthood. If you don't have a primary-care doctor you can search for a clinic near you at Yes Means Test (http://yesmeanstest.org/) or the Center for Disease Control and Prevention (https://gettested.cdc.gov).

■ EXERCISE ■

If you have been diagnosed with a sexually transmitted infection or disease, why should you disclose? There are actually a lot of reasons. By disclosing, you are establishing safety for your partner and yourself. It shows that you take your health seriously and have serious respect for the person you are going to be sexual with. This also means you have mutual respect for yourself and your sexual partner. Because you respect them, you are providing an opportunity to establish trust between the two of you and you are allowing them to give explicit sexual consent. This conversation can be vulnerable, which is difficult, but recall the payoffs from the *Vulnerability* chapter. Finally, disclosing to a potential sexual partner gives you an opportunity to educate them on STIs and dispel myths and stereotypes.

You know why you should disclose, and you have decided how to do it, but when should you do it? You should always disclose before having sexual contact with another person, but otherwise it is up to you. There is no rule about if you should disclose on the first date or the eighth. You should disclose when you feel safe and comfortable. Do your best to ensure the other person is also safe and comfortable.

Now that you have decided to disclose, how should you do it? Do you recall the Pancake Talk from the *Fantasy* chapter? I recommend using this as an outline for having this conversation so you are creating an environment that is comfortable for both of you. After you disclose your STI status, allow the person to process and invite them to ask questions. You may say something like, "I know this is a lot to digest, but it is something I have become comfortable with and accustomed to. What questions do you have?"

Most people will not make a big deal out of it. A potential dating partner once disclosed their status to me and, while I had strong feelings for the person, I wasn't sure I wanted to continue the relationship. A close friend and colleague held me accountable with a sobering truth: "You aren't going to die." It helped me realize this was my issue and I chose to move forward and establish a long-lasting relationship. If someone does make a big deal out your disclosure and chooses not to continue to date you, it likely says more about them than you. An STI doesn't make you who you are. It is a minor piece of you and millions of others.

LGBTQ+

There are approximately 11 million people who identify as lesbian, gay, bisexual, transgender, or part of the queer community (LGBTQ+) in the United States. It is likely these numbers are conservative. They do not take into consideration people who are not publicly out, or those who identify under another term such as asexual or non-binary (hence the +). Younger generations are creating new identities that better suit them, so the terminology is continuously changing.

Despite being discriminated against throughout history, the LGBTQ+ community has an extensive past with documentation of same-sex couples dating back to 2450 BC. This documentation has been seen for eras in both sculpture and paintings.

In the United States, people who have identified as part of the LGBTQ+ community have been criminalized, pathologized, and murdered. Initially introduced as a disorder in 1968, homosexuality was later removed from the American Psychiatric Association Diagnostic and Statistical Manual (DSM) in 1974. It was replaced with "sexual orientation disturbance." It was not until 1987 that homosexuality was completely removed from the DSM, when it was declared being lesbian, gay, or bisexual was *not* a mental illness. Gender identity disorder was added to the DSM in 1980 but was later removed in 2013 when the term gender dysphoria took its place. While gender dysphoria remains in the DSM, it is no longer considered a mental health disorder.

In 1988, National Coming Out Day was established and now takes place annually on October 11, the same day the Second National March on Washington for Lesbian and Gay Rights took place in 1987. While progress has been made, it was not until 2013 that same-sex marriage became legal and was recognized by the federal government. It has taken decades, and thousands of protesters, activists, and riots, to help the LGBTQ+ community make worldwide progress.

Sobering statistics tell us that lesbian and gay youth are five times more likely to attempt suicide than their heterosexual counterparts. It is estimated that 40% of transgender people attempt suicide at least once in their lifetime. According to Trans Student Educational Resources, transgender women have a 1-in-12 chance of being murdered. This number increases to one-in-eight for transgender women of color. Statistics like this make coming out scary, and potentially life-threatening, for many.

The good news is there are more resources today for the LGBTQ+ community than ever before. There are books, support groups, hotlines, pride marches, online communities, and discrimination policies in place. There is new terminology for people to describe their identities, like demisexual and gender-queer. There are LGB and trans-affirming therapists who create safe and confidential spaces for people to explore their sexual and gender identity. While there is still a lot of work to do, progress continues every day.

Telling other people you are part of the LGBTQ+ community is often referred to as "coming out of the closet." Coming out is a process of understanding and accepting yourself and sharing your identity with others. The opening of this box is an intimate and individualistic experience. For some people it is easy and feels natural to let the contents out. They are comfortable with their identity and know they will have support from their family and friends. Other people struggle with their identity so much they have feelings of suicide and fear of being ostracized by their family, church, or community. The best advice for coming out is to do it on your own terms when you are ready.

Vivian Cass created a coming out model in 1979, based on her research, in which she identified the six stages of coming out. The six stages include *identity confusion, identity comparison, identity tolerance, identity acceptance, identity-pride,* and *identity synthesis.* The final stage of the model is when a person acknowledges that being LGBTQ+ is part of their identity but it does not define who they are. Despite her research findings, Cass was quick to recognize in her first publication that the model "is not intended that it should be true in *all* respects for *all* people since individuals and situations are inherently complex." She continues by acknowledging "it is expected that over time, changes in societal attitudes and expectations will require changes in the model" (Cass, p. 235). Perhaps this acknowledgment is why Cass's model continues to be used today.

One of my clients was a man who had reached out to me via email several times over the course of two years before scheduling his first appointment. Each time, he expressed despair about his relationship and his future. I remembered the synopsis of his email after receiving it in my inbox a few times, because he sounded both stuck and desperate, but eventually he did schedule an appointment with me.

Case study: Shawn

Shawn was a 39-year-old male, had been married for 13 years, and had two small children with his wife. He was also positive he was gay and had no idea how to tell his wife, let alone his children or family.

Growing up Catholic, Shawn struggled for many years before admitting to himself that he was gay. "Honestly, I've probably known since I was about 11 years old, but I pushed it aside. I thought the Devil was testing me and I was scared, so I did what I thought I had to," he confided. What Shawn thought he had to do was pray, repent, and act straight. He put this box in a dark corner and did his best to act straight, but it was not without consequences. The consequence was that for many years Shawn suffered in silence.

"It wasn't all bad. I do love my wife. I love my kids. I can't imagine my life without them. But in the last few years I've abandoned my religion and recognized I'm my own Devil." Not only was his wife unaware of Shawn's sexual identity, but she also had no idea Shawn had abandoned his faith. They continued to go to church each week and sent their kids to a Christian school. The life Shawn was leading was taking a toll on him mentally and emotionally. He was depressed and shared he had gained weight.

Shawn spent the next few months in therapy pulling that box out of the dark corner and coming to terms with his sexuality, what it meant for his identity, and what it might mean for his future. He processed years of shame and guilt that had infiltrated from his religion, utilizing the exercise from the *Vulnerability* chapter. He had not realized how much of an impact his upbringing had on him and the implicit messages he received from his elders about sexuality, marriage, and faith.

In order to let go of these hurtful messages, he realized that, *"The primary task of coming out is to redefine one's identity so that what was once seen as an aberration is no longer seen as disgraceful"* (Olson, p. 81). Shawn embraced this concept and spent sessions developing his own sense of self, creating realistic expectations about coming out, and focusing on his own autonomy.

Once Shawn had gone through the first four stages of Cass' model, he was ready to have the Pancake Talk (from the *Fantasy* chapter) with his wife. Shawn made the choice to talk to his wife at home, feeling confident he could navigate the conversation.

Unfortunately, he had relied too much on his own experience of growth from the last few months and did not take into consideration his wife's reality. His wife thought they lived a happy marriage and she relied strongly on her faith. The conversation quickly turned hostile as Shawn told her about his sexual identity and his views on religion. His wife kicked him out, calling him a "gay asshole" and putting two-by-fours across their front door. Shawn was devastated.

The next day she let him back into the home and conveniently pretended nothing had ever happened. "It's been three weeks since this happened, and we have not talked about it since," he confided. Shawn was beside himself and unsure how to proceed. He was scared and nervous to broach the conversation with his wife again, but he also knew he could not continue pretending to live in this alternate reality. Another three weeks passed before Shawn suggested his wife come to therapy with him so I could act as a mediator.

When Shawn brought his wife to therapy the session was tense, but it was not hostile. Shawn said he was not expecting his wife to meet him with acceptance yet, but he was hoping this time she would listen to him. His wife was emotional and repeatedly said, "I just don't understand," through choked tears.

I was able to validate her and create a safe space while she attempted to process her own reaction. She admitted she had been processing it for the last six weeks but would become so angry, overwhelmed, and sad that she would shut down quickly and go into "robot mode." At the end of our session, I suggested she seek out her own therapist so she could process her emotions and determine how to proceed.

Shawn continued seeing me for individual therapy because, while he had processed his own sexual identity, he now needed to process his wife's emotional state. It was difficult for him because she was not supportive and often said hurtful things. He acknowledged his wife felt betrayed, the same way he felt his religion had betrayed him so many years ago.

Eventually, Shawn moved out of the home and the couple proceeded with a divorce. There were a lot of sessions Shawn spent crying as he mourned the loss of his prior life. There were also a lot of sessions when Shawn expressed relief and liberation, as he finally felt free from the shackles he had placed on himself for so many years.

Some people choose not to come out, just as Shawn had chosen for many years. They fear being ostracized, losing their family and friends, being kicked out of their homes, discrimination, and possibly assault or death. In many parts of the world, it is not safe to come out. It is important to acknowledge that coming out is a *very* personal decision and process, one only you can make.

Case study: Brandon and Kendra

Brandon and Kendra originally came to see me a few years ago due to a desire discrepancy. The couple met in college and had been married for ten years. Brandon worked for the post office and Kendra was employed as a hospital social worker. They had no children, by choice, but led an active life hiking, camping, and swimming at the lake with their two dogs. For many years, Brandon had suffered from depression and anxiety, which in turn affected his libido. Kendra was frustrated with their sex life, but also sympathetic to Brandon's mental health. We spent about a year working through this and they utilized exercises from the *Low Libido* and *Sexual Scripts* chapters. After a year, they got to a better place in their relationship and found a sexual routine that worked for them. They continued to come to therapy just to talk through life stressors.

During one session, Brandon shared the couple had an interesting discussion over the weekend. It was a box that had been forgotten about, but Brandon recalled liking girls growing up.

"That sounds pretty normal," I stated.

He elaborated though, "I liked them, but I didn't have a crush on them. I wanted to *be* them." After clarifying, Kendra and Brandon shared they had a conversation about gender roles and how they fall into them, but also defy them. "It was just an interesting memory," Brandon concluded at the end of the session.

For a few months, nothing more was brought up about the subject. Then one day, the couple came to therapy and Brandon shared he had been thinking more about this memory. "I started doing a lot of research on trans people," he shared. "I don't think I'm trans—" he started.

Kendra finished his thought. "—but he is obsessed with reading about what it means to be trans." We spent the session discussing what Brandon had researched, what resonated and what didn't.

The conversation was evolving. During the next session the couple had a story to share. "Well, this weekend I ran out of underwear. So Kendra suggested I just wear a pair of hers. And I loved them. So we went to the store and bought more in my size," Brandon shared with a smile. Kendra smiled too, validating Brandon's experience.

Within a month, Brandon shared they were transgender after all. I affirmed this and checked in with Kendra to see how she was doing. "As a person, I'm fully supportive. As a partner, I go back and forth." Kendra identified as heterosexual, so being with a woman was something she was still processing. She had started to see an individual therapist and was using that time to talk through her own sexual identity.

Soon, Brandon began to identify as Brandy and had started hormones and laser hair removal. Brandy began to process in therapy how to come out to family and friends. The couple had a gender reveal party with all of their close friends and Brandy felt loved and supported. This gave her the courage to start sharing she was trans with family.

The couple came out to Brandy's family first and then to Kendra's family. Many of their family members were shocked and said cruel things to the couple. Family told Brandy this was a phase that could be solved by going to church. Kendra was encouraged to leave the marriage. While these comments were very hurtful, the two found solace in doing this process together as a team. We were able to spend time in therapy talking through all the different reactions, and how to draw boundaries within these relationships.

One of the most difficult decisions Brandy made was to come out at work. Working at the post office was a male-dominated field, and she was nervous about losing her job due to discrimination. She reached out to her supervisor to schedule a meeting. Luckily, Brandy's supervisor was not only supportive, but reassured her job security. This can be an unlikely occurrence, as gender identity is often not protected in discrimination policies.

Interestingly, but perhaps not surprisingly, as Brandy became more secure in her gender identity, her depression and anxiety alleviated and her libido increased. The couple began to have sex multiple times a week, which hadn't happened since they were in college. They continue to come to therapy to discuss the hardships of being together in a conservative city, but have worked through many challenges as a couple and remain happily married.

While no one can predict how others will react to you coming out, it is a turning point for most LGBTQ+ people. Studies have shown coming out lowers stress levels and reduces symptoms of anxiety and depression. Coming out about your gender or sexual identity can literally mean better physical and mental health. It increases self-esteem and feelings of worth, will allow you to be your authentic self, to be a role model for others, and to create a support system within the LGBTQ+ community that affirms your identity. The exercises below will help you navigate the coming-out process.

■ EXERCISE ■

Perhaps you have not come out yet because you aren't really sure what to come out as. There are so many identities and labels, which can be wonderful if you find one that helps describe how you are feeling, but also overwhelming trying to learn alphabet soup. It is normal for this process to take months or years before you feel completely comfortable in your identity. You may feel confused or anxious while you figure it out. The neat thing is that our identities are fluid. If you find a word that works for you today, but does not work for you in a year, that's okay!

How do you determine the right label for you? Are you struggling with your gender identity or your sexual identity? Both? If you feel safe writing them down, try journaling your thoughts and answers to the following questions. If not, think through them and consider discussing them with an LGBTQ+ affirming therapist.

- How long have you been questioning your identity?

- Have you ever been attracted to someone of the same sex?

- Do you experience sexual attraction at all?
- Do you feel comfortable in your body?
- How do you feel about your genitalia?
- Who do you fantasize about sexually?
- When you consider going on a date with a man/woman, how do you feel?
- When do you feel most comfortable in your body?

■ EXERCISE ■

If you are ready to come out to others, how exactly do you do that? Why are you ready to come out now? Who are you going to tell? What will you tell them? Where will you tell them? When will you tell them? It is important to consider these basic questions so you can feel comfortable and confident when you come out, even if you are scared and nervous when you do it.

Remember our Pancake Talk from the *Fantasy* chapter? This is really important to implement when coming out. It creates a safe space for you and the person you are coming out to. Coming out should be done on your terms in a way that feels good for you.

■ EXERCISE ■

If you are reading this because someone you love is LGBTQ+, how can you be supportive? Your first reaction is crucial. However, if you did not react as you wish you would have, it is not too late to offer an apology and be supportive now. Sometimes people have their own experience of shock and misunderstanding. You can get your own support to process your emotions, or wait until the person is in a place to support you while you support them. Here are a few DOs and DON'Ts when someone you love comes out.

- **DO** offer your support.
- **DON'T** judge.
- **DO** ask questions.
- **DON'T** treat them differently.
- **DO** continue to include them and invite them places.
- **DON'T** tell them it is "just a phase."
- **DO** listen.
- **DON'T** make it about you.
- **DO** offer resources if they want them.
- **DON'T** out this person to others without explicit permission.

I'VE NEVER DATED

Data from the Centers for Disease Control show that, on average, people lose their virginity at age 17. They have also found most people choose to have sex before marriage. What exactly does that mean? What is sex? Does it mean a penis is inserted into a vagina? Does it mean a person who has engaged in oral sex? Did they have to give *and* receive oral sex to have had sex? Does it include anal sex?

Definitions quickly go out the window when trying to define what sex is, or is not. As you noticed in the chapter on *Sexual Scripts,* people in the field of sexuality are striving to change the meaning of how we explain sex. It is about so much more than intercourse and includes intimacy and connection. Perhaps for definitional purposes, we can agree that having sex means to engage in oral, anal, or vaginal intercourse.

Regardless of your sexual identity and how you define sex, about 12–14% of adults between ages 20–24 have never had sex. This number decreases to 5% for adults between the ages of 25–29. By the age of 44, only 0.3% of Americans have never had sex. It is unclear if reasons for not having sex in the United

States are related to religion (celibacy), sexual identity (asexuality), or lack of prospects.

According to my clients, there are many contributing factors for not having sex, including social anxiety, a lack of interest in dating or marriage, only socializing online as part of gaming communities, being focused on school or a career, low self-esteem, trust issues, or lack of opportunity to meet people their own age. They may lack the social skills to ask someone out on a date because they have never gone on a date. For example, if a heterosexual man was focused in high school and college on their grades and academics, and are now in a male-dominated career field, they may be unsure how or where to socialize with women. Many situations can cause anxiety about dating.

Most of the people who come to my office because they have never kissed someone, dated, or had sex, are men. Many of these men have social anxiety. Some of them still live with their parents. If this describes you, that's okay! First let's unpack what social anxiety is and is not, so you can begin navigating dating or having an intimate sexual relationship.

According to the *Merriam-Webster Dictionary*, being anxious is "characterized by extreme uneasiness of mind or brooding fear about some contingency." Basically, being anxious is a state of mind where a person feels uncomfortable and hyper-focuses on everything that could go wrong in a situation. This hyper-focusing prevents people from putting themselves into new or unknown situations.

Social anxiety is when a person thinks about being in a situation with other people, new people or old friends, and feels uncomfortable being in that setting. This kind of anxiety can prevent people from socializing, particularly in a crowded place like a bar or at a party. They may only feel comfortable socializing in small group settings or at their own home rather than in public places. It is also possible they have few, or no, friends. This does not mean a person does not want to be social or doesn't want friends, but their anxiety consumes them to a degree that prevents them from cultivating relationships. People with social anxiety may also have feelings of low self-worth, and feel they do not deserve to have intimate relationships.

Case study: Herbert

I met Herbert a few years ago. He reached out to me, at the age of 46, to discuss his limited history of dating and to talk about how to cultivate a relationship. The first time we had an appointment, Herbert made it to my office parking lot but never made it inside. I thought he just didn't show up, which sometimes happens with new clients, but he emailed me explaining he was too nervous and anxious to get out of his car. He had driven to the session but could not bring himself to walk inside. Herbert apologized and asked to reschedule the session. He wanted to make an appointment and overcome his fears and alleviate his loneliness, but he felt intimidated by years of anxiety.

Herbert cancelled and rescheduled two more times before he came to his first session. Upon meeting Herbert, his anxiety reduced greatly as we established rapport and began to unpack his history. Growing up, Herbert's father was in the military so his family moved a lot. He was the youngest of five siblings and relied on his older brothers and sisters for his social and emotional needs. This made his home life comfortable, but without their direct support, it made school difficult for him. He was incredibly shy and struggled to make friends. He got bullied. His shyness grew into anxiety over the years. By the time he reached middle school, Herbert stopped trying to establish relationships because he knew his family was bound to move again. If he was not spending time with his siblings, he focused on drawing abstract buildings, creatures, and constructs.

In spite of having social anxiety, Herbert was intelligent and passionate about architecture, inspired by his passion for drawing and all the places he had lived. Finishing high school a year early, Herbert went to college to study this passion. For the first time in his life, he found a group of friends to spend time with, and spent his weekends playing Dungeons and Dragons with them. Being younger than his peers, and struggling with social anxiety, Herbert focused his energy on his academic career and the few friendships he had cultivated.

After college, Herbert moved in with one of his older brothers. He lost touch with his college peers and found himself finding solace at his job and through solo projects. Since drawing was a passion of his and something he had done to escape boredom, language barriers, and anxiety as a child, he continued to use it as an outlet to escape from his lonesome reality. However, it also kept him isolated, as he would lose hours each evening to his drawings.

When Herbert's older brother started a family of his own, he naturally moved back in with his parents. He told himself it would only be temporary, but 20 years later he struggled to find any reason to move out. It was an opportunity to care for his aging parents—at least that's what he told himself. Herbert continued to work as an architect, and busied himself on weekends with his drawings. When he was not working or drawing, he spent time with his family. Because of his limited interests and outings, Herbert was noticeably overweight as well.

In therapy, we discussed the prospect of Herbert socializing and making friends. It was met with resistance as he stated, "I do socialize, with my family." This was true, but it also was not what he desired. In sessions, he had to be redirected and reminded of why he had sought therapy in the first place. He would express a desire to have friendships and relationships, but would then contradict himself and say things like, "I've been single for 46 years so it's no rush now," or, "I don't think I would like living with someone," despite living with his parents.

Counseling was paramount for Herbert because the therapeutic relationship gave him confidence, an opportunity to practice talking to someone of the opposite sex, to develop communication skills, to discuss realistic dating expectations, and to have encouragement to step out of his comfort zone. While Herbert's anxiety and shyness had hindered him over the years, his siblings and parents had also enabled him to rely solely on them for his intimate relationships. It was difficult to step outside of his comfort zone, and at times, to see the value in doing so. There were many boxes to unpack and recycle.

Progress with Herbert was slow because he vacillated frequently with his goals, and more specifically with his self-esteem. After several months he agreed to a social outing and went to a local bookstore for a book club meeting. He admitted he enjoyed the experience immensely as he did not feel pressured to come up with conversation and could focus on discussing the book. The bookstore did a monthly meeting and he planned to attend again. Herbert also agreed to establish a dating profile on a popular dating site. This made him feel very nervous, but he found some comfort in the aspect of it being online and not in person. We spent time in sessions discussing what he could put on the profile and I openly offered him feedback. We also did role-plays in therapy so he could practice how to ask a woman out on a date or what he would say to someone on a first meeting.

Within a few months, he had established an online conversation with a woman, who had also played Dungeons and Dragons in her youth. They chatted mundanely for a month and then she asked Herbert to meet in person. Suddenly, his anxiety overcame him and he felt "worthless" and "embarrassed" about his history. However, he was able to process these feelings in therapy and consider the progress he had made. Herbert committed to meeting the woman for coffee, at his favorite place so he would feel comfortable in a familiar environment. It had taken over 40 years, but Herbert was learning how to navigate social settings so he could control his anxiety. The coffee date did not lead to a relationship for Herbert, but it was a success for a man who had never gone on a date.

If you can relate to Herbert's story, you may also be reflecting on how the years have passed by without you going on dates or having sex. You may also vacillate between feelings of loneliness and pondering the point of dating or sex. Ultimately, there is only a point if you see value in cultivating romantic and sexual relationships. If you do see this value, do not hold yourself back from connecting with others. Sort through your boxes filled with anxiety, build boxes and fill them with your self-worth, and create new boxes by stepping out of your comfort zone. Remember the quote on vulnerability from David Whyte in the *Vulnerability* chapter? That is your motivation and your reminder that, "in refusing our vulnerability, we refuse the help needed at every turn of our existence and immobilize the essential, tidal and conversational foundations of our identity." Don't refuse help and immobilize yourself by keeping others out.

■ EXERCISE ■

If the thought of dating gives you anxiety, start with just meeting new people. There is less at stake since you are not trying to develop a romantic relationship or engage in sexual intimacy. If you can, go to a place you already enjoy. Herbert liked going to the coffee shop, so he met someone there for a date. He also enjoyed reading books, so he joined a book club. What are your interests and hobbies? How can you use this common ground to meet people?

▪ EXERCISE ▪

Are you ready to set up a dating profile? What should you include? What should you leave out? Here is a list of DOs and DON'Ts:

- **DO** put up a picture of yourself.
- **DON'T** post a bunch of group photos.
- **DO** identify your hobbies and interests.
- **DON'T** leave the "about me" section blank.
- **DO** check your spelling and grammar.
- **DON'T** post racist, homophobic, or sexist things.
- **DO** be honest about yourself.
- **DON'T** be negative and pessimistic.
- **DO** exude confidence.
- **DON'T** share too much personal information—it is public.

HOW TO: ORAL, ANAL

Different sexual acts add variety and spice, keeping things interesting in the bedroom. There are many sexual practices people like to engage in, many of which can be referenced in the exercise at the end of the *Kink* chapter. However, people are not always sure how to start doing something different, either because they are uncomfortable asking or feel insecure in their own sexual abilities.

Cunnilingus and *fellatio* are both Latin-derived terms referring to the act of oral sex. Oral sex is when someone puts their mouth on a vulva or penis and uses their tongue to lick the genitals. The term *anilingus* is also Latin but refers to licking the anus. Unlike the term *intercourse,* which refers to heterosexual penile-vaginal sex, oral and anal sex is inclusive of all genders and sexual orientations. Unfortunately, statistics for the prevalence of these practices is unknown, but the Center for Disease Control estimates oral sex has occurred at least once for 85% of men and women ages 18–44 among heterosexual counterparts.

Men frequently find oral sex pleasurable, but are often unable to orgasm from the act itself. This makes sense since the orifice is loose, while inserting the penis into a vaginal canal or anus is tight and there is more friction. Many men also enjoy some form of anal play, from having a tongue stimulate the opening of the anus to fingers or a sex toy being inserted. There are a lot of nerve endings in the prostate that provide this sexual stimulation and pleasure. Some men have a difficult time dissociating anal play from the stereotype of being gay, but many straight men do enjoy anal stimulation.

Unlike men, women are more likely to have an orgasm from oral sex because they are able to receive direct clitoral stimulation. However, many women feel uncomfortable and insecure receiving oral sex. This may be related to body image issues, insecurity about the scent of their vulva, or wondering if your partner is having fun and therefore limiting your own fun. There are some companies trying to help women overcome these insecurities, such as My Lorals, a company created by Melanie Cristol, which produces thin latex underwear to wear while receiving oral sex.

If you have never engaged in oral or anal sex but want to, talk to your partner. You can utilize the chapter on *Fantasy* to help elicit this conversation. If you have a partner who wants to engage in oral or anal sex and you have never tried it, try being open-minded. Many people feel self-conscious having someone's face in such an intimate part of their body, but if your partner wants to engage in this act it, is likely the issue is related to your own body image issues. While it might be easier to forego the act altogether, you may be missing out on a very pleasurable and intimate experience. That being said, if you try it and don't enjoy it, that's okay too. Regardless of sexual orientation or gender identity, not everyone enjoys oral or anal sex.

Case study: Sadie and Nixon

Not everyone who comes to therapy has a deep-rooted issue and needs therapeutic interventions either. Sometimes people come to therapy seeking resources, permission, and sex education. Sadie, a heterosexual woman in her late 20s, worked as an account clerk. She had recently gotten engaged and her fiancé Nixon had expressed wanting to change their sexual repertoire. The couple's routine was to have sex once a week. They typically rushed through foreplay to get to intercourse. Sadie accounted for this with a variety of reasons including, "Nixon just gets so excited, we skip foreplay. But that's okay because I don't really need all that other stuff anyway. He usually, ya know, pretty quick too."

She was shy and reserved when discussing sex and admitted that made it difficult for her to ask for sexual favors from her partner. "I don't even know what I would ask for anyway." She admitted she did not masturbate and was content with the couple's expected routine. However, she also could only identify two sexual behaviors she felt comfortable engaging in: kissing and intercourse.

Sadie shared Nixon had recently asked for her to perform oral sex on him. She admitted she had never engaged in oral sex and felt "overwhelmed" when she did research online. "I want to make him happy, so I want to learn how to do it, and how to be comfortable doing it." While oral sex is not typically considered kinky behavior, I did ask Sadie to do the exercise from the chapter on *Kink* so she could expand her definitions and limits of how she views sex. I encouraged her to discuss the exercise with Nixon so they could find common ground.

When Sadie came back the following session she said they had discussed the list at the end of the *Fantasy* chapter. Overall, they were on the same page and enjoyed the same sexual activities.

She said it helped her recognize she is comfortable with more sexual activities than she realized, such as being open to giving and receiving back massages and digital penetration. However, she said, "As the list went on, well, I would never do those things. I wouldn't feel comfortable at all." Then, with wide eyes she asked, "Are there people that *actually* have anal sex?" I normalized this behavior even though Nixon was not asking for this.

Now that Sadie was feeling more comfortable talking about sex, she wanted to fill a box with tips and resources for performing oral sex. "It's not that he is putting pressure on me. I guess I'm putting it on myself. I feel stupid, but I don't want to feel stupid." We unpacked this box and talked about why she felt stupid, and it was related to her own lack of experience.

Sadie knew Nixon was also shy discussing sex and therefore knew he would be grateful for any effort she made. She further admitted, "I don't want to have a boring sex life. I don't need much, but I don't want it to be boring." Some of that stemmed from a fear if she did not perform oral sex on Nixon, he would find someone else to do it and would have an affair. Being able to verbalize her fear and where the pressure was coming from, Sadie was able to process this insecurity in therapy and with Nixon. She reported Nixon was very reassuring, which alleviated more pressure.

To get more comfortable with the concept and learn how to perform oral sex, Sadie began by reading *Passionista: The Empowered Woman's Guide to Pleasuring a Man,* Ian Kerner's counter-book to *She Comes First.* Both are useful how-to guides for performing oral sex. She also did the exercises at the end of this chapter to lean into the experience. Finally feeling like she had control over the process, Sadie was able to embrace the idea of oral sex as an intimate experience she got to have with Nixon, rather than something she felt she had to do.

Case study: Jessica and Tanner

Jessica and Tanner were in their late 30s and had been in a committed monogamous relationship for the last eight years. They both worked at the same graphic design studio. They initially came to therapy to discuss how to be more comfortable discussing sex and engaging more openly with one another.

After two months in therapy, and doing the exercises in the *Communication* and *Sexual Scripts* chapters, they felt more comfortable talking about their sex life openly and frequently. Jessica shared they were "getting along well and I feel like this might be our last session."

She looked to Tanner and me to see what our thoughts were. Shyly, he said, "Well, there's one more thing I would like to discuss," and our attention turned to him. Tanner elaborated, "We've talked about a lot the last few months in here. I feel so much closer to you, Jess, and because of that I feel like I can finally share this with you." Nervously, he told Jessica he had an interest in her performing anal sex on him. "I don't want to pressure you at all," he said, "but it's something I've come to enjoy when I masturbate and I'd really like you to try it with me."

It was nearing the end of our session as Jessica turned toward us both and said, "I've learned in therapy not to react immediately. I'm not sure what to think so I'd like to just process it for a few days." Turning to Tanner, she took his hand and said, "Thank you for sharing this with me." After they left, I reflected as well, pleased each of them were utilizing the tools they had learned in therapy.

When they came in the next week, Jessica and Tanner said they had not discussed his request any further. However, they both felt prepared to talk about it now. Jessica admitted her hesitancy about anal sex but also said she was open to trying it at least once because she trusted Tanner and wanted to make him happy. Tanner was grateful for this response.

They spent the session discussing Tanner's fantasy in more detail and how they might navigate anal sex in a way that felt comfortable for both of them. I suggested several resources including *The Ultimate Guide to Prostate Pleasure* by Charlie Glickman, *The Ultimate Guide to Anal Sex for Women* by Tristan Taormino, and *Anal Pleasure and Health* by Jack Morin. I also suggested the exercise at the end of this chapter.

While Jessica was hesitant to try something new, she trusted Tanner and was interested in keeping their sexual routine interesting. She also knew if she didn't enjoy the experience, Tanner could continue to have his anal sex needs met through his masturbation routine.

They key to trying something new is to be open-minded about the experience. It is also essential to be relaxed, present, and mindful. Be aware of what is happening to your body and stay engaged in the experience. Performing oral or anal sex is a way to become intimately closer to your partner as you engage in both a process of vulnerability and pleasure.

■ EXERCISE ■

Before reading more about how to actually perform oral or anal sex, consider the following questions. You can write down your thoughts or discuss them with your partner. Make sure you are in a comfortable and quiet setting where you will not be interrupted as you process.

1. What encouraged you to read this chapter?

    a. Curiosity?

    b. Pressure from self?

    c. Pressure from a partner?

    d. Feelings of inadequacy?

    e. Boredom?

2. What feelings are evoked when thinking about oral or anal sex?

    a. Excitement?

    b. Disgust?

    c. Anxiety?

    d. Apprehension?

    e. Self-consciousness?

3. Have you ever engaged in oral or anal sex? Was it a positive or negative experience? Was it with your current partner or someone else? Was it consensual?

4. If you have never engaged in oral or anal sex, why not? Lack of interest? Lack of opportunity? Lack of knowledge? Fear it will hurt? Anxiety it will be awkward?

■ EXERCISE ■

So you have decided you are going to perform fellatio! What is that again? It is the act of performing oral sex on a penis. There are many slang terms for this including *blow job, sucking dick, going down on him, giving head, deep throating,* and a *blowie.* You should use the terms you feel most comfortable with.

If you have decided you are ready to try performing oral sex, consider suggesting that you both take a shower or bath to begin. The hot water will help you both to relax and it helps ensure cleanliness. After you bathe, continue the intimacy by lying down next to one another. You may start by kissing each other and fondling one another's chest and genitals. When you are ready, slowly kiss your way down his chest, using your hand to rub his thighs and fondle his genitals. You may choose to use a condom to put on his penis to protect yourself against STIs, plus it makes for easy clean up.

When you are ready, put your tongue on the tip of his penis and lick. You can use your tongue to lick his penis from the base of the shaft to the head of his penis, just like a lollipop. This gives you an opportunity to pleasure him and tease him while your tongue gets acquainted to his skin or the condom. If this is all you want to do the first time, you can slowly ease up and kiss your way back up to his mouth. However, if you would like to continue, put your mouth around the tip of the penis. Slowly move your head up and down the shaft of the penis, utilizing your tongue to elicit his pleasure. Do not use your teeth at all, unless he explicitly requests that you do so. You do not need to insert his entire penis into your mouth. Only do what feels comfortable for you.

You can use your hand to stimulate the lower shaft of his penis or his testicles. If your mouth gets sore or tired, you can stop performing oral sex, or you can go back to the lollipop lick.

Do not feel pressured to make him have an orgasm, especially the first time you do this. It is a new activity and you should only do it as long as you feel comfortable, both emotionally and physically. If you do decide to continue, or he does climax, you will need to decide if you want to "spit or swallow" his ejaculate fluid. Either choice is acceptable and you should do what you are comfortable with. Whatever choice you make, do your best to stay neutral and avoid any reactions of disgust. You may want to ask your partner to give you a warning before this occurs so it is not a surprise. Then you may swallow his ejaculate fluid or spit it into a towel that you keep at your bedside for easy clean up. If he is wearing a condom, the ejaculate fluid will be contained.

When you are done, continue to engage in intimacy that is comfortable for you both. You may choose to cuddle or you may continue pursuing intercourse. If you would like to discuss your performance, wait to have a Pancake Talk, as suggested and discussed in the *Fantasy* chapter.

■ EXERCISE ■

This exercise is geared at people wanting to engage in *cunnilingus,* or licking a vulva. Slang terms for this include going down on her, licking pussy, carpet muncher, muff diving, and having a box lunch. You can use whatever terms are most comfortable for you, but be mindful of the terms your partner uses too.

If you and your partner have decided to pursue cunnilingus, you may choose to start by taking a shower or bath together. This gives you both an opportunity to relax and ensures cleanliness and comfort. When you have finished, find a relaxed environment such as your bedroom or a couch, where she can lie down.

You may choose to start by kissing and fondling one another. When you are ready, slowly kiss her down her chest and stomach until you have reached her vulva. You may choose to hold a dental dam over the opening of the vulva to protect against STIs. When you are ready, gently and lovingly, lick. Use your tongue to lick her labia majora, her labia minora, around her clitoris, and slit your tongue in and out of her vaginal opening. Do not just lick the same spot over and over, but swirl your tongue around and enjoy the different taste and textures that her lubricated vagina produces.

If your mouth is tired or you become anxious or uncomfortable, you can slowly kiss your way back up to her mouth. If you choose to continue, you could try inserting a finger inside of her vaginal canal while continuing to stimulate her vulva with your tongue. If you are not sure if she would enjoy this, just ask her, "Would you like me to put my fingers inside of you?"

You may continue to stimulate her to the point of orgasm, or you may choose to stop and change sexual activities. Do what feels comfortable. If you want feedback about the experience, or want to talk about how it was for you, wait until the sexual session is over and engage in a Pancake Talk, as outlined in the *Fantasy* chapter.

■ EXERCISE ■

Perhaps considered the most taboo of this chapter is anilingus, or licking the anus with your tongue. This activity is often referred to as "licking the booty-hole." If you want to engage in this sexual activity you can utilize the directions and advice from the above exercise on performing cunnilingus. You may choose to use a dental dam as a protective layer between the opening of the anus and your tongue. Please note that once something (fingers, vibrator, penis) is inserted into the anus, it should not be put back into the vaginal canal until it is properly cleaned, as it can cause infections.

■ EXERCISE ■

If you or your partner wants to engage in anal sex by inserting a penis or sex toy into the anus, this exercise is for you. A few things about anal sex: know you can obtain an STI more easily, lubricant is a must, and there is no need to clean the inside of your rectum by douching or using a laxative unless you prefer to. It is extremely important that anything which is inserted into the anus must be cleaned properly before being inserted into the vaginal canal. It is also best to be completely relaxed when engaging in anal sex so the anal sphincter does not clench.

Just like other sexual activities, you may want to start by taking a hot bath to help with relaxation and for ensured cleanliness.

Find a comfortable area to engage in intimacy when you are done. You may choose to start by kissing and fondling one another.

If you have never engaged in anal play, it is best to start small, with either a finger or small silicone sex toy. If you use a toy, always use one that has a base so it does not get lost inside the anal canal. When you are ready to start engaging in anal play, slowly move your hand towards your partner's anus. Stimulate the anal opening by massaging it gently and rubbing lubricant around the anus. Ensure your partner is comfortable and relaxed. After putting additional lubricant on your finger or the sex toy, slowly begin to insert it into the anus. Doing this slowly is crucial so you do not cause any tearing or discomfort. To help keep your partner and yourself relaxed, you may choose to continue kissing one another or have music playing in the background so the entire focus is not on this act.

Once you have inserted the sex toy or your finger into the anus completely, you may choose to move it around internally, or move it in and out of the anus to offer stimulation. Some people may want to engage in oral sex or have intercourse while something is inside of their anus. Ask your partner what they are comfortable with and express your desires as well.

When your partner has tired of anal stimulation, or you decide you are uncomfortable or want to engage in other forms of stimulation, slowly remove the sex toy or your finger. Again, ensure your partner is relaxed so it does not cause any pain when removing it. Talk to your partner about the experience by utilizing the Pancake Talk. Did you enjoy yourself? Did they? Would you like to try it again? Anything you would do differently? Would you like your partner to reciprocate the act? Discuss.

CONCLUSION

Hopefully, now that you've finished the book, you have a basic guide to sexual awareness. You've had an opportunity to look at your boxes and how you filled them in your past. I hope that you have a few boxes you were able to remove from storage and recycle as you became more aware and in-tune with your sexual self. Sorting through old boxes is beneficial and helps us remember the experiences that have shaped us.

Moving forward, you now have a range of tools and resources to fill up other boxes that have been waiting patiently on the shelf. You should also feel ready to build new boxes and fill them up with messages that empower you and your relationships. New boxes will continue to appear as you embrace sexuality through-out your life.

As you moved through each of the chapters and completed the exercises, you have gained insight and awareness about yourself and your relationships. You may have noticed that many exercises are rooted in vulnerability and communication. Being able to address issues head on, first by yourself and then with others, is an important life skill to have. This opportunity to be vulnerable leads to self-awareness, which then allows us to communicate our wants, needs, and desires with others.

Another thing you may have noticed is that many of the chapters which have nothing to do with your issues *do* have exercises that are helpful in resolving problems beyond just their respective topic. Many of the exercises throughout the book, regardless of topic, are rooted in reflection to create self-awareness about your sexuality and how you perceive yourself and others. If you skipped chapters, I encourage you to go back and review the exercises. You may be surprised, for example, how exercises related to kink can also help with issues like low libido.

Until going through the chapters in this book, you may not have realized sexuality affects many aspects of our lives. The messages we receive about sexuality throughout our lifetime can make it an emotional and complicated subject. Messages from childhood, romantic relationships, and the media all end up in boxes that affect our views. Breaking the concept of sexuality down into one topic at a time can make it easier to process all of the stuff contained within our boxes. Having a better understanding of our sexuality also leads to us having a better understanding of ourselves, and how we interact in our relationships.

Even though you've finished reading the book, keep it handy for when you hit a rut and see those old boxes getting cluttered. You may not need to reread the book in its entirety, but you will want to reference the exercises throughout to help you if you need to get back on track. Doing the same exercises again in the future can have a different purpose, elicit different responses, and can have a different effect as you grow and change as a person over the years. Additionally, chapters you originally skipped may someday be relevant.

Remember, this book is not meant to serve as a replacement for therapy, but to help as a guide for working through issues and to offer a starting place for problems that are more complicated. I hope this book has served as that guide to working through issues related to sexuality, engaging in self-care, and finding empowerment. If you find you still need guidance after reading this book and working through the exercises, you should contact an AASECT Certified Sex Therapist for help.

ACKNOWLEDGMENTS

This book evolved over many years with my work as a sex therapist. I want to thank all of my mentors at AASECT, including my former supervisors Dr. Neil Cannon and Marne Wine. This also includes my forever work mom, Sheila Pomeranz.

I also want to thank the sex educators in my life who helped me expand my career and passions in writing: Konnie McCaffree, Karen Rayne, and Bill Taverner.

Thank you Aaron for helping me come up with this title before the book was even half-written.

Thank you Drew for all of your editing help, your honest criticism, and your continued support.

Thank you Dylan for always believing in me and my business endeavors, and pushing me to pursue my passions. Thanks Mom, Dad, and Fran for always being proud of me.

Thanks to everyone at Blue Line Coffee. I spent countless hours there writing, editing, and drinking lattes.

ADDITIONAL READING

AASECT. (2019). *American association of sex educators, counselors, and therapists.* Retrieved from www.aasect.org

Alzheimer's Association. (2019). *Alzheimer's & Dementia.* Retrieved from www.alz.org

American Cancer Society. (2019). *Cancer Facts and Statistics.* Retrieved from www.cancer.org.

American Psychiatric Association (2013). *Diagnostic and Statistical Manual of Mental Disorders,* Fifth Edition. Arlington, VA: American Psychiatric Association.

Baikie, K. A., Wilhelm, K. (2005). Emotional and physical health benefits of expressive writing. *Advances in Psychiatric Treatment* 11(5), pp. 338–346.

Bates, M. (2019). *X's and O's: Sexual wellness resource center for adults over 50.* Retrieved from https://www.xsandos.net/

Cass, V. (2007). *The Elusive Orgasm.* Cambridge, MA: Da Capo Press.

Cass, V. (1979). Homosexual identity formation. *Journal of Homosexuality* 4(3), pp. 219–235.

Centers for Disease Control and Prevention. (2018). *Centers for disease control and prevention.* Retrieved from www.cdc.gov

Easton, D. & Hardy, J. (2008). *The Ethical Slut: A Practical Guide to Polyamory, Open Relationships & Other Adventures.* Berkeley, CA: Ten Speed Press.

Fetlife. (2019). *Fetlife.* Retrieved from fetlife.com

Ford, D. (2019). *The Ford Institute.* Retrieved from thefordinstitute.com

Hoeger, C. & Lilla, K. (2019). *Vaginas and Periods 101: A Pop-Up Book.* Omaha, NE: Sex Ed Talk LLC.

Glickman, C., Emirzian, A. (2013). *The Ultimate Guide to Prostate Pleasure: Erotic Exploration for Men and Their Partners.* Berkely, CA: Cleis Press.

Goldstein, A. Pukall, C., & Goldstein, I. (2011). *When Sex Hurts: a Woman's Guide to Banishing Sexual Pain.* Cambridge, MA: Da Capo Press.

Gottman, J. (1999). *The Seven Principles for Making Marriage Work.* New York, NY: Three Rivers Press.

Joyal, C. C., Cossette, A. and Lapierre, V. (2014). What Exactly Is an Unusual Sexual Fantasy? *Journal of Sexual Medicine* 12(2), pp. 328–340.

Kalra, G, Subramanyam, A, & Pinto, C. (2011). *Sexuality: Desire, Activity and Intimacy in the Elderly.* Indian J. Psychiatry 53(4), pp. 300–306.

Katz, A. (2010). Man cancer sex. Pittsburgh, PA: Oncology Nursing Society Publishing Division.

Katz, A. (2009). *Woman cancer sex.* Pittsburgh, PA: Oncology Nursing Society Publishing Division.

Kaufman, M., Silverberg, C., & Odette, F. (2007). *The Ultimate Guide to Sex and Disability.* San Francisco, CA: Cleis Press.

Kerner, I. (2008). *Passionista: The Empowered Woman's Guide to Pleasuring a Man.* New York, NY: Collins.

Kerner, I. (2010). *She Comes First: The Thinking Man's Guide to Pleasuring a Woman.* New York, NY: Collins.

Kirshenbaum, M. (2009). *When Good People Have Affairs: Inside the Hearts & Minds Of People in Two Relationships.* New York, NY: St. Martin's Press.

Labriola, K. (2013). *The Jealousy Workbook: Exercises and Insights for Managing Open Relationships.* San Francisco, CA: Greenery Press.

Ley, D. (2016). *Ethical Porn for Dicks.* Berkeley, CA: Stone Bridge Press. Loving More. (2016).

Liberator (2018). *Liberator wedge.* Retrieved from: https://www.liberator.com/

Loving more: Supporting polyamory and relationship choice since 1985. (2019). Retrieved from www.lovemore.com

MacHattie, E. & Naphtali, K. (2009). *Pleasurable: Sexual Device Manual for Persons with Disabilities.* Vancouver, BC: Disability Health Research Network.

Malchiodi, C. (2011). *Handbook of Art Therapy, 2nd Edition.* New York, NY: Guilford Press.

Maltz, Wendy. (2012). *The Sexual Healing Journey, 3rd Edition.* New York, NY: HarperCollins.

McCarthy, B., McCarthy, E. (2014). *Rekindling Desire, 2nd Edition.* New York, NY: Routledge.

McCarthy, B., Metz, M. (2010). *Enduring Desire: Your Guide to Lifelong Intimacy.* New York, NY: Routledge.

Merriam-Webster. (2016). *Merriam-Webster Dictionary New Edition.* Martinsburg, WV: Merriam-Webster Incorporated.

Mintz, L. (2018). *Becoming Cliterate.* New York, NY: Harper One.

Morin, J. (2010). *Anal Pleasure and Health: A Guide for Men, Women, and Couples.* Gardena, CA: Down There Press.

National Cancer Institute. (2018). *Cancer statistics*. Retrieved from www.cancer.gov

National Coalition for Domestic Violence. (2018). *National coalition for domestic violence*. Retrieved from https://ncadv.org/

Olson, L.A. (2017). *Finally Out: Letting Go of Living Straight*. Urbandale, IA: Oak Lane Press.

Oster, G.D., & Crone, P.G. (2004). *Using Drawings in Assessment and Therapy: A Guide for Mental Health Professionals, 2nd Edition*. New York, NY: Brunner-Routledge.

Pennebaker, J.W., & Chung, C.K. (2011). Expressive writing: Connections to physical and mental health. In H. Friedman (Eds.), *The Oxford Handbook of Health Psychology* (pp. 417–437). New York, NY: Oxford University Press.

Pornhub. (2018). *Pornhub*. Retrieved from pornhub.com/insights/

Price, J. (2011). *Naked at Our Age: Talking Out Loud About Senior Sex*. Berkeley, CA: Seal Press.

Price, J. (2014). *The Ultimate Guide to Sex After 50: How to Maintain — or Regain — a Spicy, Satisfying Sex Life*. New York, NY: Cleis Press.

Recovery Zone. (2019). *Recovery Zone*. Retrieved from https://www.recovery-zone.com.

Schnarch, D. (2009). *Passionate Marriage: Keeping Love and Intimacy Alive in Committed Relationships*. New York, NY: W.W. Norton & Company, Inc.

Schweitzer, R.D., O'Brien, J, & Burri, A. (2015). Postcoital dysphoria: Prevalence and psychological correlates, *Sexual Medicine*, 3(4) pp. 235–243.

Silverberg, C. (2009). *Guide to Sexuality*. Retrieved from http://sexuality.about.com:80/b/2009/07/22/why-i-love-premature-ejaculation.htm

Snyder, D., Baucom, D., & Coop-Gordon, K. (2007). *Getting Past the Affair*. New York, NY: Guilford Press.

Stein, A. (2009). *Heal Pelvic Pain: The Proven Stretching, Strengthening, and Nutrition Program for Relieving Pain, Incontinence, & I.B.S., and Other Symptoms without Surgery*. United States: McGraw Hill Education.

Taormino, T. (2008). *Opening Up: A Guide to Creating and Sustaining Open Relationships*. San Francisco, CA: Cleis Press Inc.

Taormino, T. (2019). Openingup.net: Open relationship resources and home of the open list. Retrieved from openingup.net

Taormino, T. (2006). *The Ultimate Guide to Anal Sex for Women, 2nd Edition*. San Francisco, CA: Cleis Press.

TSER. (2019). *Trans student educational resources*. Retrieved from http://www.transstudent.org/

Veaux, F. (2019). More than two. Retrieved from www.morethantwo.com

Vday. (2017). *Vday: A global movement to end violence against women and girls.* Retrieved from www.vday.org

Watson, L. (2012). *Wanting Sex Again.* New York, NY: Berkley Books.

Whyte, David. (2015). *Consolations: The Solace, Nourishment and Underlying Meaning of Everyday Words: Vulnerability.* Langley, WA: Many Rivers Press.

Wile, D. (1995). *After the Fight: Using Your Disagreements to Build a Stronger Relationship.* New York, NY: Guilford Press.

World Health Organization. (2019). *World health organization.* Retrieved from http://www.who.int/

Yes Means Test. (2019). *Yes means test.* Retrieved from http://yesmeanstest.org/

ABOUT THE AUTHOR

Kristen Lilla, LCSW, has been helping people with intimacy and sexuality since 2010. She is an AASECT Certified Sex Therapist, Sex Educator, and is currently one of only four dually AASECT certified supervisors in the world. An internationally featured speaker, Kristen has been quoted as a sexuality expert in numerous publications including *CNN, Cosmopolitan, GlamourUK,* and *Refinery29.* Her first book, *Vaginas and Periods 101: A Pop-Up Book* was published in 2019. Kristen lives and works in Omaha, Nebraska.

■ ■ ■

www.kristenlilla.com